The Salt Pit

Ruby Tsogbe

ISBN:9789988282912

Ruby Tsogbe2

Table of Contents

Chapter 1

A child was sitting on the horse grass on the small walkway between the two houses at the bottom of the village cracking nutshells and stuffing palm kernels into her mouth feverishly, seemingly oblivious to the presence of the people in the walkway until a loud scolding, staccato words struck an intrusive discord, muting for a brief moment, the sound of cooking, eating and bemusing singing in branches overhead.

It was as it is in Agudze. It was *worle* just before the sun set. There was the grinding noise of a pestle pounding food in mortar *kplakplakpla* and the smell of seared groupers and vegetable soups simmered on wood stoves in an open compound inside a home. Children ran through leafy blades near the asphalt gravel road at the top of the village. They round up billies, nannies and kids, the goats foraging on grass to return them to their pen. Two homes faced the road, and other homes lined up behind them. They were separated on either side of the street and removed recessively perpendicular to the asphalt road until they disappeared into the woods.

Devietor walked to the *akparta* (the front hall) in his *xor* (house) and went through the *hor* (door) upon waving aside the *xornuvor* (partition). He opened the *fesre* (window) away from the cooling *be* (hay), the rooftop. In the room were *apaka* (carriage) and *adaka* (luggage). He put the *abaka* (basket) on the floor sill. Inside it was some *akatsa* (porridge). There was more of it in the *ze* (clay pot) on the *mle* (cooking hearth). He gulped down the porridge from a *tre* (a calabash) to squelch a thirsty feeling, and savoured the *kale* which was a spice and the *mumue* which was the lemon that went into the preparation while the pot was still on the *mle* (cooking hearth), and the flames were fanned with *apapa*. Devietor wrapped around his waist the *samasama* (cloth), and lowered himself onto the *akpasa* (recliner); he laid his head on a *sudi* (pillow).

Devienor stoked the fire to her cooking hearth, the dry log flared and the dry branches burned, and the cornmeal sizzled. She stirred the cornmeal, working against her strength to bring out of the pot what she placed into it, but as always; some crusted on the bottom of the kettle. She carried the *akple* (moulded cooked dough) topped with soup to the room and set it on a table. The man ate until he saw the ridges in the earthenware. A drink of water from a *tre* (calabash gourd) allayed the taste of spices which his wife added to the preparation. He smacked his lips and belched in between pronouncements. The woman smiled. When he finished eating, he propped his neck and stared at the bales of hay on the thatched roof. His elbows were crossed over his forehead, hyperextending his neck over the back of the reclining seat where he had been sitting since his return from the farm. Only when it was time to eat supper did he bring them down.

Getting up *zia* which means quickly with an *adanu* (a plan) in mind, he reached for the *asawi* (a mesh) in a *kusi* (a basket), *papanu* (a towel) and *akutsa* (a sponge), this was also called *agbitsa*. Devietor opened the door and stepped onto the grounds. He strode down a narrow strip of *gbe* (grass) separating his *afe* (house) from his neighbour's *afe* (house). His arms extended over the *gbe* (grass), stretching from *asibide* (finger) tip to *asibide* (finger) tip.

Whu! a single wooden shutter panel swings outwards. Amator leaned forward and spoke excitedly, offering his greetings through the open window. Then he came out to meet Devietor on the grounds where they walked and talked time and time again. With an air of nonchalance, with fingers laced behind him, Devietor sauntered through the compound, moving towards another compound where bleating goats huddled in a small area surrounded by stakes. Domesticated goats, guinea fowl and chicken scuttled, strutted, bobbed, pecked and nibbled on grass and grain. People also walked gingerly on cobbles placed obscurely on the patch of defoliated dry earth on the ground. Flocks gathered around the herbage in stalls. He peered inside the pen. Savor was feeding his goats with grass.

Savor called out from the stall, "Is that you, Devietor?" The sound of his footsteps had given Devietor away.

"Yes," the Devietor replied. Asked about the wellbeing of Savor's wife and children, Savor returned the greetings.

"I will take two of the billies, your best ones," he pointed out his choices, two hairy adults. It was time for another celebration. Devietor continued, making gestures, laying bare his thoughts.

Savor opened his arms wide and moved stealthily towards the goats. They skipped and ran blindly, bumping their sides into the fence. He reached out and grabbed them. Focusing his attention on one then the other, he forced them into a corner and grabbed the animals by their hind legs. Savor roped in each billy. With a sailor's knot around its neck, he led it out of the stall and handed it over to Devietor.

Devienor was eyeing a smouldering log in her stove when Devietor returned. A woman must have a smouldering log at all times. The flammable fuels used for cooking, firewood burning quickly, broken dry branches and stems burned along with the slow burning logs; dry husks and shells of palm fruit stoked the fires. The active *mle* inspired cooking. *Ami* (oils), *borbor* (softly boiled beans), *akakle* (plantains mashed and mixed with roasted corn flour and boiled in tender fresh plantain leaves) and *alayiyi* (seared meat) were products of unattended slow-cooking that happened overnight. As she was moved, she covered the open flames with a pot filled with dry beans and water.

"Please," she said, "I don't know whether you remember that we have to visit *aveme* (forest) again or not." She reminded him politely that the sweet sap draining from the felled palm tree was collecting in a gourd. They set out to finish their tasks in a forest that was far from the village.

Chapter 2

Kukunor was sweeping at dawn when footsteps broke through the measured intervals of bundled spines striking the ground. The sound grew louder and louder as Kuku walked towards home. Kukunor continued swiping the floor hard with the thumping drawing nearer to her. Kuku stumbled over the broom. She gasped.

"Oh, *baba* (sorry). You have returned early from the farm. Are you well?" The mother asked.

"I am fine," Kuku answered his mother. He walked into the inner chamber and stepped out again, moving towards the farms. Kukutor stepped out when his son was out of earshot and lunged at his wife asking why she didn't ask where he had been, "Didn't you hear the lone man procession coming from that direction to this house?" He drew imaginary lines with his arms.

Kukunor played it off, "Not exactly. My back was turned."

"I think he left the house in the middle of the night. He was returning. Of all the things I fear, I fear sleep the most. My body was drained, and I lay helpless. I think we should select a woman for him. I think he likes Devie. Childbirth, puberty and death are accepted as routine. Outdoors, marriages and funerals are institutions we celebrate ingesting water, herbs and spices. People dressed in light, coloured or dark clothing share hereditary, heritage and heirloom. They can do little about routine. They encourage participation in rites of passage, and frown on shirking rituals."

Kukunor expressed her concern, "You don't think that is where he has been?"

The father recalled a conversation he had with him, "No. He has said she is a good woman. It is the human tendency towards eugenics, you know, for the powerful to find the beautiful."

Amator heard every word of his neighbours' conversations. The story animated him. He was like a plant animated by rain and sun rays anytime he came across any impropriety. He mulled over what he heard: "This sort of matter is to be kept a secret."

Kukunor set aside her broom. She scooped some *borbor* (softly boiled beans) from a pot on the open wood fire. She added *akakle* (ripe plantains mixed with roasted corn flour and boiled in tender plantain leaves). When Kukutor requested his favourite food, she warmed *fufu* and soup which she kept overnight. Kukutor ate and left the house with urgency, walking towards silhouettes at dawn. He returned from his farm at midday, when the sun became too hot to bear. Kuku was in tow.

#

On seeing the frog couching beside a boulder in the house, Devietor ran out.

Frightened, Devienor cried, "Yie!"

Amator heard the commotion and ran over to Devietor's house.

All was well. Devietor had a cassava stalk in his hand. He told Amator that a frog was croaking in the house, and he checked for snakes lurking nearby, but they weren't.

Amator tapped Devietor on the shoulder and gently nudged him towards Devienor. He whispered, telling them the strange things happening in his neighbour Kukutor's house, "You and I have something to build," Amator concluded. He went home after visiting for only a little while.

#

Devie was youthful, stocky and large; her radiant neck creased. She fastened her garment with graceful spontaneity and leaned over the cooking pot, pulling it between her feet, but all the while she was complaining that the *sasa* (patchwork) made for an ill-fitting outfit because she was unable to properly cover up her chest, Devie tugged at the folds of woven material above her mammaries, getting ready to wash pots. Devienor said lumps on the chest should keep a woman from going topless, and added that too much of the material was being hemmed in, so Devie folded the edges over, leaving none of it at the seams, and the tie was a better fastener of things, then she stretched her wraparound sheath down to her knees and allowed room for easy movement of the legs. The cooking utensils were coated with a residual mixture of fish and oil, and she scrubbed what stuck to the cooking pot with a wet *luffa* sponge. With sponge and water, she began to work at removing the residue inside the earthenware pots before her.

"Devie, your father wants to speak to you," Devienor's voice drew her daughter's attention, and she hurried towards the reclining *akpasa* (reclining seat), wiping her hands along the way. She and Devietor sat down to build something for their daughter. Parents didn't tell their children what to do, they gave them the choice of one option. It was what had been formed in their minds even if it was not understood. She spoke first, saying, "I was sixteen when I was given away to a male, but for two years, I wouldn't let him touch me!"

Devietor cried, laughing, "As for you," he turned to his daughter, "Have you given any thought to marriage? You know you're growing old."

Devienor drew her seat closer to her husband, until Devie was facing her. She batted her eyes fiercely. Devie didn't capture her mother's message. She had never seen her mother spar with her father over anything in public. She parented a child without ambition, and stayed a step ahead with animation.

She wore a smile and grunted. Devie gave her mother a quick stare.

"No, I haven't," Devie answered.

#

It was on the way to market that Devie met her purpose in life. She walked ahead of Devienor and her aunt Navi on the way, and she enjoyed her moment of solitude walking alone. At first, the emptiness imposed desolation on her until she filled her mind with images of her destination when her eyes opened to a blue arched dome, and she realised that every likeliness of livelihood would present itself inside the dome. Devie saw a farm and sat on a buttress root among the crops. The plantains and bananas looked similar, and their stalks were indistinguishable. People carried bananas on platters, and they sold and ate raw fingers of bananas. They arranged plantains on the ground, but they always cooked plantains before they ate them, sometimes they cooked them before they were ripe. Vidzienor sold *koliko*. *Koliko* was made from root crops and plantains. She sat on the root and waited for her mother and her aunt there.

#

"Eyake!" Devienor exclaimed and stood on the gray clay *kpodzi* (mound). She dug it up and hauled it. Devietor cut down trees and turned them into poles and stakes. He picked up a palm sap that was fermented, pungent and tart. Devie bore firewood on her head.

#

Devietor distilled the milky sap and turned it into clear pure proof alcohol, then he erected a shed with some of his neighbours because compounds overflowed when relatives gathered together to perform a rite of passage. Mama made sure that sheds were built for special events. She told people to stay away from extreme weather elements. Anyone who ignored these warnings found out that he or she had to stay in bed and be nursed back to health on the light porridge everyone called *akatsa* or *koko*. She chuckled at the thought.

The scent of trees and herbs filled the air as Mama ground herbs together -- *afla, dzeveti, wodogbugbo* basil, *tso, kale,* and *mumue* which grew at the *gborto* (outside the compound) and generated a sweet smelling aroma in the warm climate. She discovered that some of them had medicinal properties as well.

Devienor gave her stove and the wide *anyigba* (clearing) around it a fresh coat of clay, then she washed some edible leaves, *gboma* the bitter tasting leaves and *singli* the slippery ones. *Gboma* was added to other vegetables to make sauces thicker, while *singli* was added to okro soup to give it a very slippery feel. Oil could be eaten plainly with boiled beans, but the occasion called for soups and other heavier foods, vegetables and starchy foods that were only eaten at bedtime.

"Devie," Devienor called her daughter, "Take out your clothes."

Some things were passed on like logs burning in the fireplace through searing heat and cold harmattan nights. Clothes were passed down from generation to generation. The colours of these attires matched the colours of blooming flowers and budding leaves, scintillating as sun rays, transcendental in value and price, clothes made from cotton so polished that they were shiny, supple and soft as silk. They were handwoven. There was a *fomenu* they dressed in to celebrate an event. She was airing theirs. Expensive hand woven materials were aired in the shade rather than washed, because they were meant to last for generations. Everyone was putting away clothes that they used for mundane tasks like farming and household chores, those were made from jacquard leftovers. They were either faded or stained clothes. A mature fruit was useful in any state. One must know these things.

Try to explain *kornu*. Is it a neck thing or a lift thing, a cleansing thing or an enlightenment thing? If it is a clan thing, it is also called a *sa* thing. How about a *sa* thing, is it a tie thing or a cleansing thing? Anticipation and waiting are gifts that one must enjoy.

Chapter 3

This was before people pushed creaking doors, sweeping brooms and kindling logs. The cock stirred Devietor now and then. When footsteps broke through the silence, Devietor dashed for the door. The man entered the compound wearing a dark red hunter's smock and a greenish herbal facial mask. He exchanged pleasantries with Devietor on their way to untie a billy from a tree. Devietor dragged it; the man reached for it and dragged it outside the compound without uttering a word. Devietor followed. He doubled in his footsteps and caught up with them. The man scanned the surrounding bushes, found a suitable spot and removed the soil with a long knife. With a wave of his hand, he motioned to Devietor to bind the limbs of the goat and lay its head across the hole. The butcher slaughtered the goat and blood oozed onto the ground. The man walked away in silence.

Devietor walked towards Devienor's room calling out to her, "Is our mother there?"

"Yes."

Devienor placed a pot on the cooking hearth with clay jambs. One by one, she added spices to okra, tomato and green leaves stewing in palm oil. She then added bitter *gboma* leaves to thicken the sauce, and thinned it with slippery *singli* leaves. Palm oil kept its flavour from manipulation and spiked in the flavour of the best *fetri gboma* soup she ate with *amor kple.* Devienor added firewood and fanned it with woven leaves to fuel the flames. To achieve the most palatable without inundating the taste buds with excess was the essence of cooking. The people of Agudze found a distinctive flavour they worked to bring out of food. The meal was an art they appreciated with their senses and put into their bodies three times a day with clean right hands. A few occasions called for heavy meals, vegetables and starchy foods that weigh on the body and make it to relax.

"You are well accomplished," Devietor commended her.

Mama made soup and oil from palm fruit. She separated the husk from the pulp with water after she cooked and pounded the red fruit, -- when the extraction boiled and the water separated from the oil. She turned the bland liquid into edible soup with added vegetables and spices, and removed the red oil to use later. She changed "red oil" to "fire oil" by dropping red hot stone in the red oil before removing it from the fire. The fire oil had a potent flavour and it did not spoil.

Mama removed flesh from dry shells of red palm fruit as well as coconut palm fruit. After roasting the flesh, she ground it. The butter was bitter, but when she boiled it with a large amount of water, a golden oil rose to the top. The residue was also bitter and solidified when it cooled. It had become a useful fuel.

#

Devie woke up and seeing the silhouette of trees, she immediately picked up a water pot and walked to the stream to fetch water.

"Agoo," Devienor walked to her daughter's room. She announced her presence and pushed open the door with her hand.

"She has gone to the stream," Devietor cried out, but not in time to stop her from entering the room.

A dress lying on top of a stack of wooden boxes caught Devienor's eye. She picked it up and stuck it under her arm, rolled into a small bundle. She replaced it with an upper garment (blouse) and some *dzonu* (necklace beads). The garment, which is shortened to hip-length, is worn over a skirt that is wrapped around the legs, completely covering the mid-riffs to the ankles.

Devie returned. She put some water on the stove and warmed it to rinse off the caustic mixture of plantain and oil she rubbed on her skin to cleanse it before slipping into the outfit her mother left on the top of her *adaka* (luggage).

Her mother walked towards the room reciting, "Libation clothes.... Dress up in libation clothes. You should remember to put a second cloth over your outfit. The second piece of clothing was a reminder that she had made the leap to *ame* (a mature person). "How is the dressing moving along?" Devienor asked as she helped her daughter zip up her blouse. After that she walked out.

Devienor walked back to the compound and disappeared into the shrubs lining the path. She was not thinking about plants particularly. At that moment, she was walking towards her mother's house.

Some girls were walking towards Devienor on the path and she greeted them from afar. Her scowl changed into a smile when she asked, "How are you?" The girls looked up at her and responded, "We are well". Devienor cringed as she continued on her way. The girls from her village fidgeted, rubbing the back of one hand over the other and touching big toes on the heel of the other foot as she spoke to them. Devienor walked past the adido tree in front of her parents' house without realising it. Navi was sweeping around the adido tree when she noticed her sister striding past the house, so she called her and asked about her wellbeing, "How is the house?"

"We are there," Devienor responded.

Navi turned towards the house and called out to her mother, "Mama, your granddaughter is ready."

A wiry and muscular patriarch gathered together yards of cloth around his waist, draping the hanging ends over his shoulder and walked a little unsteadily through the compounds, breathing the smoke of wood fires and the smell of breakfast foods mixed with the fresh morning until he was first to arrive at Devietor's house. His dressing dates back to ancient Grecian times.

Mama sat with legs stretched out and crossed over. Her arms and hands trembled. She clasped and turned her gold chain *korxla* (necklace) around her neck. A head scarf covered her head, and she pulled it away from her forehead. Her outfit was made up of three wrap-around skirts on the bottom part of her body, and a lined upper garment. The three bottom wrappers not only concealed her womanhood, they also created the illusion of large hips as she stood. Her arms moved lower to strap her sandals around her ankles and picked up a purse that was full of accessories. She stood up. Her rueful smile was defiant, and it took some goading to get her away feeling satisfied for she was as particular about her appearance as she was at age nineteen. She carried her style.

Devienor walked into mama's room and greeted her mother saying, "Dada, morning to you."

"Good morning. How is the house?"

"We are well. I want to thank you for cooking."

"Feeding you is not worthy of thanks. You should have had enough help to prepare the dough to go with the soup. How is the child, are you getting ready?"

"Yes. I will now return."

#

Just as shimmering sun rays began to squirt through tree branches and fall on rooftops, a procession marched towards Devietor's house. The people carried gifts in basins that were balanced on their heads. They had *kpo* (yards) of cloth that were neatly folded and arranged to look like flowers growing out of very large old *agba* basins that had been left outside. They also carried earthenware pots, pans, wooden utensils, and spices, and everything sprang out of large new brass *agba* basins. Devie's husband was among them.

"They are here." "Are they here?" "Where are they?" "Here they are." The people of Agudze were animated by news as they were animated by salt, the clear crystal that worked like rain and sun rays. People began to gather at Devietor's house after ascertaining that the suitor had arrived. The space on the benches that lined the four walls of the *akparta* were occupied, some people stood outside in the shade.

Devie hid in the bedroom. In time, she would be brought out to be identified. Her face would be covered. Her husband's test of knowledge was to pick out her legs in a lineup of sorts when girls picked at random were disguised, their faces and shoulders were concealed, and presented to him. If he failed to recognise Devie's legs, the ceremony would be called off. This would be done after negotiations and gifts were taken. Everything was meant to be a surprise, but terms had been agreed on, so the suitor's family brought predetermined goods to give to the woman and her relatives, even so they would scream and gape and feign surprise as the woman's family made demands during the proceedings.

Devie's friends entered her room. They were surprised to see that she was wearing the upper garment and an ankle-length skirt instead of a frock. The dress was cut below the waistline and did not extend to the knee. She wore it over an ankle-length straight wraparound skirt. Devie noticed their looks of surprise.

"We are black african christians!" The girls cried in unison.

"My mother is not seeing it," Devie whispered with an air of nonchalance. Devie was ready to receive many more visitors and gifts.

Devienor welcomed the girls to the gatherings, shouting, "*Mi tso, mi tso na ame dzro,* stand up, stand up for the strangers." Young people stood up to make room for the guests to sit on benches.

Adufie joined the inquisitors. For a moment, he aired his jumper tunic, cocked his head and looked around. Then he made a declaration of marriage. He opened the ceremony by filling up the *tre* (calabash, a sectioned gourd, which he removed from the mouth of the *aha go* (gourd filled with palm wine). He coddled the calabash with both hands and shot the drink onto the ground at his feet, to the sides and to the front while synchronising along loquacious utterances to the ancestors. He emptied the contents of the calabash onto the floor. Pouring libation on the ground for the ancestors was central to every process.

Devie's grandmother arrived to sit with her. She broke the silence with some advice, "You know, a woman must take care of herself...," yet a feeling of sadness accompanied the joy she experienced for the reality of mortality was obvious. Giving away a child in marriage was establishing the next generation, and she was preparing to move into the twilight, "The only door I own is always open to you. Come always, anytime, live with achievement, watch and read inspired memory, sleep on vision, pray with wisdom, feed on love, joy, peace, longsuffering, gentleness, goodness, faith, meekness and temperance. One must prepare to live every day..."

Three times, a woman went to devie's room and returned with a young woman whose face and shoulders she concealed. Devienor cringed every time a girl came out.

So it happened that Devie married Vidzie.

#

Devie's friends were excited at the close of the ceremony. Kay grumbled, "I was thinking the palm wine was being poured for our drinking when he began pouring it all on the ground, and I almost fainted. Our choice of drinks was limited to that aliha which was sweet."

"Some said they made it from crushed germinating corn. It was caramelized sugar which gave it colour and flavour," Zoe offered some insight.

Kay sneered, "The idea of drinking boiled germinated corn might be suitable for this occasion, but I imagine the ancestors would have preferred not to get drunk on palm wine."

"As for me, I enjoyed the food," Zoe snapped.

Kay was adamant, "The smoked fish they used was big, but did you notice that the bigger the fish, the softer it became once it was pulverized twice? I heard they fried fish before stewing it, and smoked fish before boiling it. And those tomatoes, onions, green leaves, garden eggs and okro were either stewed in oil or boiled. I heard they ate vegetables cooked and raw fruits, and they made butter and oils from all types of nuts. Grains were pulverized, especially corn. Dry corn was soaked for three days, milled and soaked again for another three days."

Sally became curious. "Why?" She asked.

Zoe whispered, "To achieve the maximum levels of fermentation, I presumed. Sometimes they roasted corn first before milling it, but they mixed it with everything from beans to plantains. What a variety of foods to enjoy! The types of food they ate in the mornings and afternoons were different from the types they ate in the evening. They hardly ate during the night. They encouraged children to save some of the food they ate after the sun rose, midday and before the sun set. I used to come home with her when we vacated the school during the middle of the school term. While I spent the whole weekend at her house, she woke up early to sweep the house and get water from a stream. I had to go with her. When we returned, her mother had yams peeled and boiled. She asked us to grind some tomatoes with spices, and added some fish that was grilled on the coal in the hearth to warm it up, perhaps because it was smoked fish....

Funny thing was the same ingredients were used for the evening meal but were prepared in a different way. What I discovered was that in the evening, the cooking was more elaborate, more time was spent boiling the fish and spices with a few extra vegetables thrown in. What was eaten as moderately chopped pieces in the morning were mashed up by pounding with pestle in mortar in the evening. It did not matter, be it yams, cassava, cocoyam or plantain. There must be green plantains, of course. Only hard-boiled food was pounded in a mortar."

"Perhaps, there was not enough time to prepare such meals in the morning," Sally suggested, "On the other hand, they might have trouble digesting breakfast foods in the evening. I remembered her mother telling me once that it was too late to eat beans in the evening."

Kay groaned, "All the talk was about tradition!"

"Yes. Traditions solve problems. Things are different for her now. She must have standards. Every effort will be made to make life enjoyable for her. There is a problem only when she does not enjoy it," Zoe whispered.

Kay wasn't convinced: "They took pains to placate. The colours of the clothes were taken right from the middle of the spectrum of light."

Zoe rebuked her, "They were bright clothes. How can you say such things? Must we have a reason for everything we do?"

Kay retorted, "Was that why they gave her all those gifts?"

Zoe was visibly shaken, "She seemed to enjoy all the things she was given. Did you see she was smiling throughout the event?"

Kay had a reason, "She was coy."

Zoe said softly, "Let her continue to enjoy herself. One must not only be prepared but be ready for marriage. There is a certain amount of suffering to be anticipated when she subjugates her feelings or adopts restrictive qualities and is self-regulating. She is disposed towards commitments to the community's values and traditions, like not taking medicine when she is ill and such. There is a certain amount of preparation that goes into it. We should all be made to take tests and pass them. It is something of a transition. She will have to wear a second wrap when she steps out of her house. It is much like wearing a sash to traditional functions from now on, not unlike us.

Kay relented but she had a few questions, "You are right about preparing. What did you say she is not living her life? Is she not thinking for herself? Did you see how they treated the man? It was as if they were taunting him to make him go away. A man is something to behold, his physique can be terrifying at times, but we are built to complement each other, so I don't understand why some people have such a terrible view of marriage."

Zoe had a few questions also, "Who said she was not? I heard Kuku wanted to marry her, but someone lied about him. There were rumours about him and Sika. If he wanted to marry Devie, why was he always in the company of Sika?"

Sally reflected on what she heard: "I am going to include lying on the list of sins to be delivered from. I feel bad for his loss. Thinking about the Lord's prayer, the idea of evil should extend to cover all of the prohibitions mentioned in the covenant on mount Sinai. I had not taken the fact of lying as evil seriously. I always had death in mind when I said that line. Coveting is even more difficult to determine. How does a person make a relationship work?"

"I don't know," Zoe said, "What don't you want to hear others say to you?"

"You have foul odor," Sally answered.

"What else?'

"You won't share?'

"Share what? What else?"

"You have used up all of the soap."

" It depends on how old the soap is."

"You sleep too long?"

"It depends on how long everyone sleeps," Kay interjected.

"You talk about me to your friends," Sally added.

"It depends on what you talk about," Kay interjected again.

"You are nasty to me," Sally squeaked.

"That is two out of ten. The rest are about traditions. Sally, you are right that she is not thinking for herself. She shouldn't have to think only about herself, but she shouldn't only think about the man either," Zoe bellowed.

Kay was caught up in a reverie, "Do you think she will have a white gown marriage ceremony? It will be accompanied by another round of cooking. Seriously now, the church is called the bride because of what happens at events like this. Such a celebration! As for me, I am a black african christian." She recited:

"Life is lived in the realm of senses.

Adjectives are seen in forms with concrete lenses.

I am looking for that colour Black to see it to no avail.

I am looking for that earth Africa to touch it to no avail.

I am looking for that worship Christian to feel it to no avail.

Black, african, christian are words that are abstract, and they leave me as a construct.

My bloodline is neither Black, African nor Christian."

Zoe was incensed, "Honestly, I don't see how that relates to marriage, unless you consider it a basis for forming a community and expanding that community. An unseen community is built on unseen spiritual gifts, but a visible community is built on spiritual fruit."

"What about batons and flags and swords and staff?" Sally asked.

"Parents bear them all," Zoe replied.

#

Kukunor spoke frantically to Kukutor after *Adufie* walked away, saying, "We have to find out who he sneaks out to see. He will not agree to marry anyone if scandal breaks out."

"Will he agree to marry anyone now?"

"I think I will water the ground just as Devienor and Vidzienor have watered the ground, I am going to speak to Sika's father."

"He may turn you away if he is not a sound sleeper. Besides, if Kuku does not know what to do before he will not know what to do after."

"It is a chance I have to take. Both of the children are fools. We have to make them understand that."

"Yes, they are immature. I will send Kuku away to one of those big schools."

"No. He will find another victim. That will make us irresponsible adults"

"Then we have to deal with the scandal."

"Sika will have to be sent away."

"What is more, I heard it was one of her great grandmothers who discovered the substance that causes miscarriages. You would think people who are aware that looking at certain creatures causes skin discoloration in babies would be careful, but some people may be having miscarriages by design."

"Kei. You are perpetuating a vicious rumour, but it is a fact that neither Sikanor nor Sikator is concerned with identifying the cause of change in the behaviour in a child. They don't have the benefit of discussing issues over conversations. A child must be given a dose of salt."

Kukunor was silent leaving Kukutor guessing what she was thinking.

#

It was *worle* in the evening when the people of Agudze sat on their verandas and eagerly waited for Devie and Vidzie to step out together for the first time. They came out walking through Amator's compound. When Amanor saw them, she ran into her inner chambers and returned with *dzonu* strings of beads to tie around their necks and wrists. She gave articles of clothing and jewelry and adorned Devie and Vidzie. Devie's grandmother made sure that the neighbours had enough items to decorate her grandchild. They made the celebration a true community affair.

"Aww, Devie and Vidzie," Amanor composed a melody that instant, using congratulatory messages as lyrics. She waved the items until she was close enough to roll them over their heads. "*Ayefro me konu o,*" she cried and swayed, waving a kerchief as she followed the couple into other compounds. Young boys and girls stood along the sidelines to ogle their victory walk. Adornments were lavished on the couple from one end of the community to the other.

Devie and Vidzie walked through Kukutor's compound to return to Devietor's house. Kukutor serenaded them. He said, "Each heirloom is made from cloth. Each cloth is made from swatches. Each swatch is made from threads. Each thread is made from cotton balls. This cloth is unlike others. This cloth is made for longevity. This cloth is made for sharing. They go through phases of exposure and effect, bud and blossom, undergrowth and overgrowth, wilting and withering, overgrowth and undergrowth. It all depends on exposure to light. They sing a song composed by the dry ground, anyigba. It wasn't so long ago that the sun left them untidy during the harmattan season. The renewed state only lasts for so long, but the wasted state must come before." Kukunor doused the couple with talcum powder.

Chapter 4

Calm serenity was restored to the village the next day. Of the structures erected, only the cooking hearth remained. People gathered the palm fronds, wooden stakes and logs which were the *agbador* (sheds), and they became cooking fuel.

Dusk was on their minds when the people of Agudze followed the clay road from the (*gbeme*) bush at the *gborto* (outskirts) of the village. They had strutted through *adame* (fields) where there was *gbedadafo* (wild grass) to *aveme* (forest). People made their *bome* (farms) there. They made farms on *kpodzi* (mounds), on *todzi* (hills), in *agudzi* (beyond the horizon) by *tsito* (the river).

No one had been able to grow food since rain stopped falling in Siamlom which was in July. During the harmattan season, palm fruits continued to grow. They grow every two months, growing in perpetuity; seedlings pop up to replace dying plants. Coconut palm kernels slowly fill up with juice. After a while their inner linings developed into pulp. The pulp became hardened meat as the juice was absorbed. People bring home heads of oil palms now and then. They cut coconut palms from their trees as well. Crops were never completely decimated by the *pepi* (cold dry harmattan winds). Cassava stalks remained viable and tendrils sprung from the nodes. Fruit and vegetable seeds were also viable when they were dry.

Twice a year, they planted crops to supplement perennial foods. When the rainy season arrived, people used any land that was not covered by buttress roots to grow food. Togbe put together tomato beds and yam mounds during the *nufaxi* (planting time) which coincided with the *tsidzanorli* (rainy season). There was early rainfall and later rainfall. He planted and waited for *nunexi* (harvest time) which took another two months.

With the coming of the rains, distinctive leafy blades appeared. They grew flowers and fell. Vegetables and fruits grew where flowers were. They waited two months. Togbe said two months was the most important duration. A person could live without food for two months. He said that at the end of two months, there would surely be food.

They dug the ground to uproot bulbs. They pulled or cut ears of corn from the stalk, and cooked them succulent fresh on the cob or as dry kernels. The peppers and tomatoes grew in gardens and people had easy access to them. Trees grew and shed like skin, fruitful varieties of palm trees bloomed in the background. *Gboma* and *singli* had inedible pods and roots, but the leaves were tasty slippery gumbo. They were preserved and planted for their leaves. There were root crops like cocoyams in abundance. It was true that every crop had a miniature variety, plantains came with bananas, coconut palm with oil palm, the soft yam that was called *kooko* with cocoyams, yams with *nkafu*, even corn had millet.

#

Vidzienor prepared to lift her load of yams. She stood up and stretched her arms downwards until the muscles at the back of her forearms began to contract, then she bent her arms and contracted the muscles at the front of her arm lifting the load. She stretched the muscles at the back of the arm again to put the load on her head.

Footsteps came from behind as Vidzie walked towards her. "I am on my way to help," he said.

"Aaaah," Vidzienor released a soft slow grunt. Vidzie helped her lift the load the rest of the way. His mother carried condiments in the cup of her elbow. She was careful not to thrust out her neck like a bobbing cock as she looked to see to it that Vidzie also helped Devie put the rolled cloth on her crown to protect her hair and scalp from getting excoriated when she carried a basket of yams on top of it.

"We have already unloaded the firewood under the shed," Vidzie added and walked away.

"Are you ready?" Devienor asked.

"Yes," Devie replied.

Market days were celebrated quint-daily, that was every fifth day after the last one. The road was full of people who were walking to the market, and the humming sound of their conversations was interrupted now and then by loud greetings and responses spoken in unison. Devie walked on the road to the market as a married woman for the first time. She walked with her mother-in-law by her side. Her clothing was a whitish wraparound skirt and short dress. It was one of the gifts she received. The colour of the clothes of the marketers betrayed their status. They wore white or light blue signifying nursing, black and brown signifying bereavement or all other colours covering the spectrum of light from orange and green to magenta for ordinary days. Their engagement with each other was always based on the spot on which they found themselves.

Devie peeled, sliced perfectly sectioned yams. Plop, plop, plop, the translucent pieces of yam she dropped into a wide aluminium pan over the wood fire in the *mle* stove floated the hot oil. Steam pressed against her face and neck. The hot oil sizzled and fizzled as water drained from the yam. They turned white then yellow.

"Mhuu!" Vidzienor drew Devie's attention to the browning edges of the yam. Devie stopped stoking the fire and scooped that batch with a strainer. The spectacle invited curiosity and hunger that continued day after day.

#

Devie's mother stopped by to make conversation. She watched and did not take a person's word because little was offered. She had the same conversation every market day saying,

"Your disposition has been revived. What have you been eating?" She asked a rhetorical question which made Devie smile. Then she turned to Vidzienor and said softly, "Since the rains have been delayed, have you found any good yams...." Devienor began a chat with Vidzienor while Devie minded the food.

Navi set up her table with fish and tomatoes that were preserved in cans. She neatly stacked them one on top of another, built into pyramids. Ever since her return from school in the coastal city of Ademai, she had taken the lorry there often to get mackerel, sardines, and tomatoes and returned to sell them at the market. People preferred to buy dried or seared meat and fresh tomatoes at first. Slowly, they began to appreciate the taste of canned fish, and simply ate the fish out of the can. They added thickness to their sauces with canned tomatoes. Devienor moved towards Navi with a look of satisfaction. She said that Navi's wares were suddenly becoming popular.

"Yoo."Navi acknowledged her words of encouragement.

Devie slowly became acquainted with strangers at the market as she spent all day listening to conversations, arguments, gossip and plans.

Kukutor spoke loudly at the entrance of the market. There was no gate. The first people to arrive sat nearest to the edge. Those who followed fell behind, leaving enough room for buyers to move around. Kukutor spoke some words in English and rattled others that were incomprehensible once in a while. He held a Bible over his chest.

"Ohay," Vidzienor turned to Devie and wondered why a man would want to speak in any language other than the one he knew.

Some people walked over from the other side of the mountain to sell and buy here on market days. Their village celebrated its market days on the third day after Agudze's market days. Devie eyed the stack of yams on top of their large wooden pallets.

Others arrived early as well, with women carrying vegetables and fruits and men drawing their flock of sheep and goats. Market day after market day, they sat through the afternoon heat under the protection of large tree shades or sheds covered with palm fronds. These were poor conductors of heat. Traders returned in the evening unless rain clouds sent them scrambling to get home early. They ate and chatted, exchanged wares and made promises to each other throughout the day.

Until now, Devie had never been this early in the market and knew people only by what they sold. She knew the *azitor* who sold groundnuts, the *kpelitor* who sold corn, the *tetor* who sells yams and so on. For weeks she called people by what they sold, until one day, Vidzienor asked,

"Do you ever wonder whether or not people get tired of being known by what they sell, when they have names? Take for instance *azitor*, we used to call her Komlanor. Komla was the toddler she strapped to her back. She had older children who visited once in a while, and they called her Gamelinor."

"So what is her name?"

"You have to learn to be more attentive to those with whom you travel, otherwise you will become creative and descriptive when you talk about others."

#

Vidzienor invited Devie to Anyanui to shop for yams. They set out at dawn and travelled on the mountain. The plants were scant but varied, and the stones were many, they covered the landscape. The birds flew freely, resting frequently on branches. There were antelopes who were startled at the sight of people and galloped, disappearing behind the rocks. Devie wondered why there were no antelopes in the village. She said nothing, because a child was not expected to initiate a conversation, perhaps she would find the answer one day. She focused on big rocks as markers to help herself remember the path. As the youngest person on the way, she was expected to walk ahead of Vidzienor.

They arrived in Anyanui. Traders had their yams arranged on their wooden platters. Vidzienor picked up enough yams to last for two more days, because in the interim, she sold koliko under a shed that was built by the main road.

Chapter 5

Togbe had a single cotton tree among his variety of crops. One day, Devie asked why there was a lone cotton plant and Togbe responded, "It is not so." He told a story that left Devie flabbergasted. It was what was left after the British destroyed his crops. Devie could not believe her ears. The British were friends, or so she taught. She remembered seeing a photo of the young queen among her grandmother's favourite belongings. Noticing the look of disgust on his granddaughter's face, Togbe explained that it was not their fault. He explained that it was the Germans who started warring with everyone.

But what had Germany's war with Britain to do with destroying crops thousands of miles from the other side of the ocean? As if to read her thoughts, Togbe clarified his answer, saying, "They destroyed their properties wherever they could find them." Togbe told her about the day priests arrived to visit the people of Agudze. He said they dressed in outfits that were overflowing. Togbe found the distinct attires most uncomfortable. They were not particularly illustrious. The clothes were fabricated with machines rather than in the weavers' looms.

They had something important to say. It was chaos. They found the established order to be idiocy. They superimposed an established idiosyncratic principle with institutions. They were busy, busy, busy offering blessings, sacrifices without law, without clarity.

Some elders asked questions such as, "Is this new idea ...an idea that will make us last until tomorrow?" Togbe's father's fears overcame him. "It was a good thing that the strangers did not speak the language," Togbe concluded with a smile.

#

Children went to school. They stood up when the bell struck seven and walked towards the chapel. They didn't return until the sun positioned itself for a reversal. They missed the activities that took place at home. It went like this: The ding of the church bell followed the cockcrow, and the bell ringer struck a string of chords after the initial two strikes. Worship service started and the children got ready to go to school. When the priest, wearing a flowing gown with an upturned collar, walked from the back pews towards the front, children dragged themselves out of bed. They bathed and sat on a stool waiting for their mothers to set before them earthenware stuffed with food: Boiled plantains and stewed cocoyam leaves spiced with pepper and flavoured with salt. They drank water with their food.

"School begins at seven o'clock!" A mother would shout at her child.

Mama struggled to deal with this new idea, and kept the children at home, "You say your school begins at seven, but you don't tell them when to walk out of the house. It is like expecting a cock to crow before it's time." Mama always said, when she was their age, children gathered around the *mle* stove and ate roasted palm fruits. Oil palm trees grew food inside as well as outside their kernels. Pulp was extracted from husks and used to make the basic ingredient of soups, otherwise the pulp was boiled and oil was extracted from it. Spices and vegetables were added to take away the bland taste of sauces. All of the dried meat that was either inside or outside of kernels produced oil. Palm oil and other oil that came from the kernel after it was roasted and milled into butter, albeit bitter to the taste. The butter was boiled with water, oil rose to the top and was scooped up. Coconut oil like palm oil did not solidify but palm kernel oil did.

The children often got to the bell tower and stood by to watch the bell ringer pull the rope for the last time.

They wore school frocks without long skirts. Some girls were not from these parts, but they resided at the institution where Devie took classes. They spoke a language that was common to them but unknown to her, but Devienor insisted on their learning the greeting.

#

Plant shooting from beds contributed to the school's landscape. They lined the sides of the school yard. They were especially colourful, small blue, pink, yellow and purple flowered plants with small tuberous roots that were neither edible nor useful except that they held the morning dew that watered the earth. Thistle removed, the grass was cut low on the field where children posed just like the adults doing stretching exercises in front of them.

The commotion going on at the schoolhouse invaded the village. There was a meeting, and all of the members of the community were invited to attend the meeting, so the fathers went to the meeting.

Children gathered together at the school compound. They engaged in several different activities. Some children sat on the floor in a large square room with their legs crossed. A man dressed in black khaki shorts and a white shirt with short sleeves stood in front of a blackboard hanging on the wall. He took a piece of chalk that was beside a baton on a table and began to write on the blackboard.

The children peeked through wide wooden window frames, their little arms shot up in the air now and then, all except two of the children who were sucking their thumbs and some others who were covering their yawns with hands placed over their mouths.

Listening was not new. People here were familiar with sound, they heard single, dual and triple beats and pauses, stressed beats. They also spoke. The mother who had a toddler or a small child also had a favourite expression, "Do you hear?"

Reading was a new idea. Reading was new. Eyes could not see sound, it was the ears that heard it, and mouth and tongue that must form it. Reading was like listening, repeating and walking to different beats in sequence, harnessing energy to continue. This was not different from singing, and they knew how to sing songs. However, singing was not the normal way people talked to each other or about each other.

#

"*Woezor, woezor,*" master Yawo shouted when he saw Kukutor walking into his office. Master Yawo walked around his desk to welcome Kukutor, and helped him to one of the two chairs that he set against the wall. "So you are braving the heat in the sun, I see," he chided albeit with humility.

Kukutor basked in conjured up images like an aroma diffusing *gbe* (herb) basking in the scent of its leaves. After exchanging greetings with him, he told the headmaster a story, "On the racetrack are competitors and foes. Conversations between them must be waived with a flag that indicates a competitive friendship weighed on an uneven scale of winner and loser. He is a friend, the one whose red tail lights give warnings about twists and turns in the way throughout the darkness. He is a foe, one whose angry-looking arched brow headlights signal the approach of a menacing phantom. One must have a competitor on a lonely road, be it friend or foe."

"What is the matter now?" Master Yawo asked as he twitched in his seat and held his hands tightly between his thighs.

Kukutor continued, "Eating the fruit is the truth the snake encourages. Don't take fruit is the truth God commands. "The fruit that will open your eyes is the truth, the snake asserts. The fruit that will open your eyes is the truth God withholds. You will die is the truth the snake denies. The tree of life is the truth the snake omits. Trespass is the truth the snake perpetuates. So the issues of fornication and abortion are only symptoms of a problem. The problem is mistrust, seeking answers in the wrong places."

"I have been hearing rumours....." Master Yawo tried to goad the reason for his visit out of Kukutor.

"So you have heard? With the excuse of the enemy. Umm. We are made to learn, chase illusions that are elusive, sparing expenses that are expensive, stoking fires that are fiery until they are over, but it is never over. When something is said in several ways, and the same thing is heard in several ways, there sure is more to learn in every way. These are cases to be studied: Psychology, Sociology or Philosophy. The case is made for prayer to the author of ideas that are borrowed."

"I may have heard something. However, I am not sure whether or not we are speaking about the same event."

"Perhaps, I should explain it. Anayitor has paid me a visit, perhaps to file a complaint, I don't know. It has come out during our conversation that Anayi has made a retort, perhaps to correct his mother or to demonstrate to everyone how much he knows, I don't know, but his mother has only asked him to sit up, and he gives a response. He responded that he was not in PE."

"Is that really true?"

"It is just as I say. I asked Anayitor. Anayitor responded enthusiastically. He is still a child, and children should not speak like that! I asked him how old he was!"

"Exactly!" Master Yawo said in utter surprise. What do we do now? We have taken note of the day, month and year in which all the children are born. Especially now, they have to be able to tell how old they are when they are asked. The old criteria for qualifying children for admission to school comes in handy. Besides, parents have always noted the differences in age among their children by treating them differently. They cannot just call an older person without putting a title before his or her name. The hand comes in handy. A hand that does not extend beyond the earlobes is not allowed to write on a blackboard. You can tell a person is intelligent by looking at the arrangement of lines on the palms, but you cannot bear maturity in the palms."

"We are overlooking an important solution."

"Don't let them out of your sight."

"How do we do that?"

"I will call a meeting since I am the headmaster, I will demand that the school hold a meeting with the community to discuss the behaviours of children."

"Don't forget to mention that I, Kukutor, have walked into the office of the headmaster to give a report in a loud voice saying, "Anayitor says he is uncomfortable with the way that girls and boys are speaking to each other and to their parents."

"I hope you are not asking that boys and girls be separated at school. We encourage discussions among boys and girls. Perhaps, they can find something idealistic for impressionable minds."

"Too much learning makes life

impersonal. That is an excuse to distort their values with extraneous activities, and keep them from working on their individual ideas."

"We are teaching principles and laws that children don't have the time to experiment with."

"We have sayings, *lododowo,* ourselves. They are not learning any of those. What type of lives are they going to live?

The thing about fringe benefits is they are laced around the basics like reels on wheels. Basics are put out of focus when they are acquired for the sake of benefits."

"We can keep them engaged in physical activities. Values are regulated by our ability to achieve them, otherwise, we would not have an earlobe test."

"What do we get from education? Is lack of self control caused by a disease on the brain? I believe the time will come when individuals will be studied to see how the mind is working. Abortion and fornication, lying, greed and fear will no longer be a mystery. It seems all we are doing is speculating. On the other hand we may be acting out expectations of an authority figure. Is it possible that some people cannot grasp these expectations? Perhaps, the expectations are not ground into a person with effort and time. Perhaps the expectations are wrong."

"That is why our ancestors shun families with individual problems. It takes bravery to try to restore values to a people, but is it our place? We do restore people who have boils and wounds to wholeness, assuming the whole person is a work in progress. Let us do more for the mind."

"You keep them here all year round."

#

Kukutor returned home. Kukunor was grinding spices on grinding stones. She looked up to welcome him home and noticed that he was hesitating to walk to the *akpata*.

"I think there has been a little too much salt added," he observed.

The name salt bore the connotation of animation. It was a name that was given to pepper sauce and to food. Pepper sauce had added ingredients such as tomatoes, onions and sometimes ginger in addition to salt. These ingredients were always stashed in a small basket for storage. They were ground up in an earthenware pan that had circular ridges. The ridges helped to rub them into fine paste with the help of a small wooden pestle.

"Bring a seat here for your father," Kukunor told Kuku.

"The belly holds more food for a lot less time as we grow older. I have a well cultivated taste in spice. First, I am allowed some sugar. They add a taste of salt, before long, I am eating pepper, I don't know when they sneak in ginger, cloves, basil, things growing above the ground or under it. We learn that those who eat salt have sharp minds. We are building a school for adults," Kukutor gave his wife some information, sitting on his *akpasa,* "We will keep them occupied and we have to sleep lightly."

"He is an adult."

"It is only when we say so. If there is a scandal we will lose our clout. It is expected of us to maintain our integrity."

"I think I have to stay awake. Maybe he will stay if he knows we are awake."

"Your health and productivity will be affected."

"I will take it as a matter of raising him."

"That was what one of the teachers said. He said we should keep our eyes on them. That was what your parents did."

"How do we do that if they are away at school? The dressing is *penttee* (painting), greasing the hair and face and in between the toes."

"If it had not been for the dressing, she could not compete with Devie."

"But if our son sees her that way, he does not see a woman. I am not even sure that he sees a person, all he sees in them are workers if he draws comparisons. This one has more prowess, that one doesn't. What will he do if she does not bear children if that is what he expects of her?"

"The man believes in courtship. He takes time to worship. He cries tangled bows like boughs on a gazebo. He took pruning shears on Sunday morning and fishing rods on Monday morning. He trims his boughs on Sunday morning and takes his wife fishing on Monday morning. He keeps his religion in tradition. Adam fails to see his weakness."

Kukunor was silent leaving Kukutor staring at her and perhaps wondering what she was thinking.

#

Sika and her mother *kle* (met) Kuku and his mother at the market. The mothers greeted each other. Kuku was silent and looked the other way until they walked past Sika. This did not escape Sikanor's notice and she related the incident to her husband on her return homem "You know when a child is concerned. It is true, people have seen them alone."

"Now, about Ham. If only Noah had not planted the grapes. If only Noah had not made some wine. If only Noah had not drunk some wine. But it is about Ham. If only Shem and Japheth were the first to see their father naked. If only Shem and Japheth had left Noah to his oblivion. If only Shem and Japheth had left Noah naked. But it is about Ham. If only he had honoured his father. It was the only law which applied. Since he didn't honour his father, he had to honour his brothers," the father's anger was apparent.

"She is not concerned. As far as she is concerned, she is glad he does not bother her anymore. She must have known that what he was doing was wrong."

"Adam sings about his prowess, of ownership of place and companion to name at will, but Adam fails to rule his passions."

"She went along with it, and showed no respect for us."

"I say there is no understanding of things."

"Perhaps things have changed. One day, there will be the usual procession of the suitor's family. I hope it is not too late for this life.

"They may be born again if they embrace a different idea. This book is full of intrigue, of people interacting, of people interfering, of people interceding, of people discovering one who has access to all. Ananias and Sapphira are related to each other. They believe the message is to repent together. Together, they join a community of believers. They obfuscate the objective of the community together, they die together."

"Which book?"

"The way the strangers explained it, the Bible story contains a fable, but it is not a fable. The story contains an imprecatory psalm, but it is not an imprecatory psalm. It is a story about a son who obeys a parent. We are flocking to ways defined, preparing for viewers to refine, until we hear through discourse, they have an end as a matter of course. Adorning God is the everlasting way."

"Which book?" Kukunor asked him again.

#

Kukutor's lantern burned night after night. His books were strewn all over his side table. They were books about the subtlety and courage of animals and people. He memorised some of the words.

Kuku walked to his father's door, but did not enter. He listened but did not hear the shuffling of book pages and so he imagined that his father dozed off with his light on. He walked away to return after the sun rose. His father watched in silence as he walked away from the house day after day.

Kuku began to keep his lantern burning at night and he spoke up, "Why do you keep your light on?"

"It is because I cannot sleep," Kuku replied.

"Rest is not understated. It is the law that one should rest and be refreshed. Refuge is finding rest, not sleep. Refuge is laying the mind aside and not sleeping. When the very air and space are tackling, find refuge in the life you are given," his father's wisdom came to the fore.

"Yes, but sometimes some thoughts appear to take over," Kuku gave voice to his inner struggle.

"What do you do with thoughts? You make plans. You discuss them with your parents, some plans are not achievable, some are not good to achieve." His father beat about the bush, but continued, "Do you have a woman in mind?"

Kuku could not talk about that. He grabbed one of his father's books, and walked away. When he returned, he displayed a poem that he had written on the table and read aloud, "From talk to speech to book to film, we learn to shtick with schick media. Recording history and reliving it in the future. Robbing the present of proper procedure for upbringing emotions and hopes in pedia. Disregarding propriety. With regard to persuasions without common ground. Find new issues to resolve or find someone from an old issue to absolve. We establish relationships and adapt to each other, but soon after we abandon each other, we denounce each other. Celebrating triumphs in living and emulating evil by following. Writers are our sages. We are children, students, and followers looking forward to their presages. We all have mouths, we have something to say, you read my book and I'll read yours."

"Don't be a lazy writer. Be sure to check grammar, spelling, punctuation and ideas," his father advised him.

Abruptly, Kuku walked away from the house again. His father followed him and asked, "Are you going to write?"

"No. I am going to watch the sun rise," Kuku responded, "Consider this a good life, under skies, on space harbouring creatures rooted in land, this clean air under trees, being in the company of creatures great and small. I can live in a glass house that is constructed with mud bricks. I see through it, I breathe through it. It is a sturdy glass house. It withstands wandering creatures great and small."

Kukutor walked back to the house and woke Kukunor up speaking excitedly, "Paul returned, his blindness removed, he has studied for three years, he is willing to teach. But Paul is defined by the blindness of the crowd. They ran from him, stoned him, imprisoned him and killed him. I think it is time we gave him his own piece of farm."

"But we still have to keep our eyes on him. He hasn't admitted to seeing a girl. He has been seen with Sika. They walk alone and talk to each other. I have been told that she has been vomiting and getting the chills, but they say it happens in the afternoon sometimes, perhaps," his wife whispered.

"That must be gossip. What do you think they are doing?"

"He simply could have asked us for her hand."

"He hasn't."

"He must do as he is instructed. He will have to be guided through life every step of the way. He won't be the first."

"You know all fingers are not equal. We have to think about the market going forward."

Chapter 6

As the man approached the market wearing khaki shorts with a safari shirt and holding a baton, Amanor sounded the alarm: "I think the tangas are coming." Fear gripped women in the market when these representatives of the town council came and collected levies imposed on them. No one kept books because they could neither read nor write, so there was no record of transactions. They thought of stories to tell when they saw them coming. The women began to whisper among themselves.

Vidzienor shuffled her feet and muttered, "I have just arrived. I haven't made any sales." Awonor suggested it was the police because he was holding a baton, but that story was also laid to rest because the police uniform had slightly different features, the shirt worn by the walking squad was dark blue and collarless. By then the man was moving through the market, greeting the women. He was identified as the man who looked at the school gate. Stopping at the shed where Devie was frying *koliko*, he handed her a letter and walked away.

#

Vidzie looked over at the compound from the front window, waiting for the women to return from the market. They returned to chattering as they walked.

"I want to show you the difference between *puna* and *avadze*," Vidzienor told Devie as they walked towards home.

Devie knew yams. Yams tasted sweet, bland, and sometimes left *akalo* (alkaline) taste in her mouth; they crumbled easily when her mother cooked them. Once in a while the tail end of a yam left a bitter taste in her mouth. The type of yam Devienor used was distinguished by its looks. It was slippery whitish, firm, almost translucent starch contained in earth sheaths. Her mother-in-law kept yams in their best conditions to make koliko, but their quality was average.

Devie slid the letter on the window sill while exchanging greetings with Vidzie and walked to the fireplace to unload the remaining yams. Vidzie read the letter. He explained to Devie that the school was inviting her to cook for staff and students, so she would have to travel to Ademai to learn how to cook while her expenses were paid for by the school.

Devie declared, "I am not leaving." A moment later, she broke into a wide smile and shouted excitedly, "I am coming," just as she skipped across the compound. Vidzie watched as she skipped all the way to her father's house.

Vidzie opened his mouth to speak again as she skipped across the compound, but he did not give voice to his admonition, "We don't have money," until he spoke to his mother.

His words jolted Vidzienor, and she had to think quickly, "We will not give up this good idea. This should not spell doom for the marriage," she said.

These were times when the problem of money had not reared its ugly head, when snakes were one's worst enemy and a stranger was a sacred messenger.

"Be patient, Vidzie," his mother said calmly, "No problem is insurmountable."

"Aloo?" She looked at her husband eagerly expecting a nod of affirmation.

Vidzietor grunted.

"Aloo?" She asked again.

He imagined hearing aloo repeatedly to the point of nagging and he said so. It was as if she had injected hope into his body when he added, this may be a good thing and spirited his way around the village spreading the news from elder to elder. He didn't need to not express his fears, because his care was theirs, and what they called "coba," the newly introduced copper coins, began to flow into the house as gifts in anticipation of a journey together to the city by Devie and Vidzie.

Devietor was the first to arrive at Vidzietor's house. He twisted his mouth a little because he heard stories. "Are you sure?" He asked Vidzietor.

"It is as they say," Vidzietor replied.

Devienor and Devietor began to spend much time at Vidzietor's house. Devienor especially would spend her free moments with Vidzienor. Kukutor explained to Devietor that life in the city was a life behind walls. More of their people were getting involved in processing and distribution of what they found naturally. Some of the products that they brought on the *torwhuu* made it to their market on market days. She was going to live as a stranger but she would be taken care of.

Devietor tried to assure his wife, but Devienor was not sure that was a good idea. Navi came to mind, "She will return safely, but as a different person."

Mama often broke into song singing, *"Na mewor de ke O 2x. Na dudor mewor de keo. Na du dor kakpoor fo nye dzi lo* (Na has done nothing. Poor Na has done nothing. Poor Na has fed my stomach.) Yes. They will return to bury us," Mama's voice broke in lament as she sang. She lurched forward, steadied herself on her feet, straightened her knees and back and continued, "Birds are aware of the loss of a soul in a community. *Hedorameku*'s cry at dawn indicates a soul has departed. Birds are aware. I am standing on it."

"We will send news to the city," Navi assured her.

Mama took her eyes away from the hot mixture momentarily to look and complained, "One by one our young people leave to work in the city, but all fingers are not equal, so they all don't have to leave, neither do they have to become identical in thought, action and speech? There is a way things ought to be done, and that is all they need to know." She was unusually kurt.

"I would think one leads to the other. They will return."

"It used to be that they went for a brief period of schooling."

"They will return. They have to find the materials with which to work. We get and send letters through the Post Office"

"They will come when their grandfather is no longer with the community."

"Being with the community has a different meaning."

Mama said yooo softly and looked at her daughter from the corner of her eyes with a smile on her lips.

#

Whuu was the sound a vehicle made when it sped through the air at dawn, and that was what the people of

Agudze called a vehicle. It was the thing that travelled along the outskirts of Agudze to go to the coastal city of Ademai.

Devie pushed her slim figure into her old school dress and strapped on her school sandals. Vidzie also wore his school shorts and shirt. The community gathered to wave goodbye to them. Everyone enjoyed the light tomato soup which Vidzienor prepared with the lamb that Savor offered with *fufu*. *Adufie* drew some water from the pot and poured it on the ground to ask for their protection. Devie carried the dry fish and oil sauce, and Vidzie carried the bags as they set out to board a vehicle on the road going to Ademai.

Chapter 7

Navi sat under a large *adido* tree beside an earthenware bowl of plantains dulled by heat and served with mashed cocoyam leaves, tomatoes, peppers, onions and dried fish stewed in red palm oil as she heard footsteps approaching and pulled her wraparound skirt between her legs. She continued to separate the rafia and the sandy leaves which were used to wrap salt and wound the flexible reed around a stick. Devienor arrived and pulled up a seat next to her since an invitation was a superficial request. They washed their right hands with water, then suddenly, a vehicle moved towards the adido tree and got so close to it that branches bent, twisted and broke.

When *Adufie* heard the commotion, he came running down the path towards the tree shouting, "Try running it into the trunk!" He realised it was Devie and Vidzie. He rushed to get a bag which Devie was carrying away from her before exchanging pleasantries with them as they walked into her father's hall.

Devienor watched her daughter in silence.

"It's the slit!" Navi said under her breath. She looked up at her sister and tried to speak, but stammered again saying, "It's, it's the slit."

Devie arrived wearing a skirt and blouse, but her long skirt was not the only open two yards of cloth that was wrapped around her legs. It was made from one yard and left an opening from the ankle to the thigh just below her buttocks. Devie was ubiquitous on arrival, sticking out among women who had wrapped themselves in cotton cloth that exposed only their shoulders with the mind to endure the heat. The men walked around with bare chests above cotton knickers.

"What is that?" Mama asked about the embroidery at the neckline of Devie's blouse. Mama's attention was focused on Devie's blouse. "It seems the necklace has been attached to the blouse." She continued while tucking her welcome *dzonu* beaded necklace into the folds of her wrapped skirt.

"It's called *jorome.*" Navi whispered to mama, then she complimented Devie aloud on her outfit saying, "Your blouse is especially fitting."

Devie twirled and began to hug everyone present while they continued to discuss her appearance.

"Why does she have to resemble the people of Alata this way? Isn't this what they do to their hair? What are you thinking? Lest anyone should say it was I who said they took joy in combing their hair, *Adufie* sneered, "She seems to have learned much. She didn't go there looking like that!

Devietor took leave to retrieve a gourd of palm wine to perform the second welcome ceremony which consisted of sharing palm wine with the dead and the living. *Adufie* tipped the calabash in three different directions, and passed the rest of the palm wine around to everyone.

Everyone took a sip except Kukutor for he insisted, "You must mean everything to everyone. It is a subject that is an object. A word that is not rehearsed in poetry. Giving to a neighbour, storing in God's house, planning for the future are all called saving."

Devietor revived the conversation. There was a premonition because Devienor stabbed the right big toe all morning, "Anytime it happens, I tell her she has stabbed a good foot."

Devienor agreed, "*Apaniapa!*"

"My wife has become a foreigner again with this talk," Devietor laughed.

People expressed themselves in foreign words which they picked up from visiting strangers. Perhaps she was trying to impress this on Devie.

"How was the journey?" Devietor asked.

Devie and Vidzie replied in unison, "It was peaceful."

Adufie continued his task, asking them why they came, "We must ask even if we know the answer. Ours is a peaceful abode."

Vidzie responded, "Neither are we carrying bad news. We have come to visit you."

"Devie, take your luggage indoors," Devietor told Devie, and she disappeared into the bedrooms with her packages wrapped in woven bags.

No one spoke for a while, but Adufie broke his silence with a blunt warning that, "There is no work here for her to do." "How long does she plan to visit? It is a crime. It is working against a parent's wishes, that is *vodada,* and not dressing properly that is *nugbegble* (destruction)."

"She was too young to remember," Navi said. She looked at her sister as if to plead on her niece's behalf. Navi remembered the reception she received on her return from Ademai too well. Devienor was silent on her arrival, and Navi wondered. She had gone away to study on scholarship from the education ministry. She returned with every intention of teaching at the local school. Wearing a form-fitting skirt that opened at the seams to expose the legs changed things. Devienor didn't speak to her for a while. When she spoke she said, "You allow your dressing to be influenced by the eclectic world of the city. It is strange and unsuitable." Navi explained that it was another element in a string of misunderstandings directed at all things associated with the residents of the city. They were considered to be lewd. She also was wary of dressing like a city girl, but after a while, she understood that it was just a cover up. What was the point of recounting stories from the past unless the reason was to repeat them? She would have told Devie the story before she left for Ademai, Kukutor the headmaster called her to his office and dismissed her. She recalled what her older sister said then, "What is good for a school child is not good for a schooled adult."

Devietor interrupted her thoughts, "A child must be told what to do."

Devienor was not to be outdone. She totally condemned the decision to allow Devie to travel to the city. "Is this a child?" She asked, "Ahh! I should have drawn a line through it."

"It was her husband who took her there," Devietor reminded her.

Devie sat on a stool in a hall that was quickly filling up with people who came to welcome them home. They threw powder at her and her husband, but after offering welcoming messages, they left one after another. Devienor also left to go to the kitchen. Then Devie and Vidzie went home to Vidzie's house.

#

Walking away from the school, Devie walked towards her parents' home. She had not only come to visit her aunt and grandparents but to offer them gifts. When she offered Mama hers, she said thank you with a smile on her face, laid the wax print on some logs beside her and continued to stir her caustic ash of incinerated dried plantain peels into overheated palm oil to make soap.

"When are you going back, perhaps I can use some of this rafia to plait your hair?" Navi asked Devie.

"Tomorrow," Devie replied.

Navi invited Devie for a conversation, "Pull up a chair. I hope you know you have to dress decently here."

Devie was surprised to learn that Navi was a teacher. Navi admitted that her books were collecting cockroaches in the cool damp wooden book where she left them several years before. She asked Devie to follow her to the room in the corner of the house and showed Devie her books. Together, they aired out the books, cleaned out the trunk, and placed the books back in the trunk. They closed it and left.

Devie asked her aunt, "I wonder what the community thinks about a woman wearing long knickers."

"Nothing! They have projected a corrupter on me and terminated the livelihood I have worked hard to get. I don't know why?"

"Why don't you tell them that?"

Navi snorted, "Perhaps, it isn't meant to be. Look at the attire ladies dress in now." Navi looked up at the mountains. Her eyes wandered until they reached the tallest mountain appearing in the distance. She continued in a manner of observation, "If you grow up looking at mountains, it may be difficult to imagine how to live life in the plains, that is assuming you are aware that there is life in the plains."

Devie laughed and said, "Life may be lived; however, people who live in mountains don't and probably shouldn't care about that. They may very well turn their mountains into plains."

"Perhaps. Perhaps, anyone can live in the plains if they learn about the environment. Knickers are for men to wear under their big wraps. Women are beginning to wear them also. It is wearing underwear as the main clothing but no one cares in the city. Men and women are adding shorter versions of knickers under their clothing anyway. That is why slits are appropriate. Sometimes, you can see the smaller underwear through the trousers also, although it depends on the type of material that is used to make the trousers. Nylons are sheer, more revealing."

"Mama says we will no longer have any use for beads. Are we going to wear beads ever again? What is the point of wearing clothing?"

#

Adufie had gifts of tubers of yams tied tightly together with palm fronds for Vidzie and his wife when he went to Vidzietor's house in the evening. "Agoo," he said, "It's nothing." He continued talking after he sat down and offered his greetings, "As an uncle it is necessary for me to know how my children are living in a stranger land."

Vidzietor smiled and called Vidzie and Devie into the hall.

Adufie gave voice to his curiosity after a while, "First of all, what is the nature of your work exactly?"

Devie answered, "It is like living at home. We sell oranges and bananas, the only difference is we keep records of the money we use."

"Money is everything. We pay for the place in which we live, we pay for water and food, so we also find a way to make money...short of stealing!" Vidzie elaborated on her answer.

Devie whispered, "It's just that some people overcharge."

Vidzie squeaked, "That depends on who can afford to be overcharged."

Devie groaned, "Sometimes, it is done indiscriminately."

Adufie demanded to know, "How does a person sell bananas and oranges without first growing them? What I gather is that the place is not an *aveme (*forest). You have only been there for a few months."

Devie explained, "We take them from those who come to market or travel to the *aveme* (forest) to find them."

Vidzienor begged, "What happens when you become ill?"

Adufie snapped, "That is just it, a person cannot afford to fall into trouble, nothing of the kind."

"That is what hospitals are for, but you have to have money in order to visit a hospital. Those who work there need money," Devie informed them. "And he has a Secretary…" Devie explained.

"*Whatery*?" Vidzietor was baffled.

Adufie would not be outdone, he shrieked, "*Secutery*."

Devie squeked, "Secretaries do what Vidzie cannot do…"

Vidzietor: "*Atsusi wu amenu*! What does your wife do when she is managing your affairs?"

Devie: offered an explanation, "She knows more…. A person must make a living…"

Vidzietor offered an insight, "It's exploiting her life!"

Vidzienor seemed resigned to their circumstances, "It is something they are used to."

Adufie snapped, "Crime! It is acting against the wishes of a parent. *Vodada,* that is sin, and disposing of a person improperly, that is *nugbegble.*"

Vidzietor asked, "How is that?"

There was silence in the room when *Adufie* sneered, "Assuming that Devie cannot do what she is capable of doing."

Vidzienor was invigorated, "We must be careful about these things. In a world in which we are largely accommodating people and things, it is time we realized when we are adopting vehicles for travelling, we must make preparations, vehicles must be married to roads, they need proper roads to strive, and people must not run them into trees. Just by looking at it, I can tell it will break down. What does it run on?"

Adufie answered, "Food."

"It is called petrol," Vidzie corrected him.

Vidzietor asserted, "I say, and I speak as someone who believes that God first creates a proper atmosphere before putting creatures in it seeing all these things that are just there, we must think about the basic necessities. That is how the world works."

Adufie snorted, declaring his disgust and realising that he needed more information. "Building on what we have to move around," he asked, "People are always looking for something new, but before long, the new becomes mundane. I wonder what is next?"

Vidzie had become accustomed to his uncle's questions, "There is something new, and it moves faster than lightning. It is called an aeroplane. I could buy one in time." Vidzie touched his fist to his chest with pride.

A surprised Vidzienor wondered if they should offer sacrifices to ablate indiscretion, "Those things are not necessary. Your priorities are getting skewed. How do you get the latest means of transportation without giving thought to the road it travels on? You must know more about these things." Vidzietor said this firmly, "I have heard enough. Come home. Skills do not help if you cannot use them." He turned around and thanked *Adufie* for his visit.

#

"Devie, I think he is suggesting that we keep our vehicle in the city," Vidzie complained about her uncle's actions.

"Vidzie, I don't know what he thinks."

"Any thinking person knows he is expressing his displeasure at the damage the vehicle has done to your grandfather's tree."

"My grandfather has said nothing."

"I know your uncle *Adufie* has said enough, but he has little knowledge, his eyes need opening if he thinks getting the best out of life means planting grains and cassava."

"If you are laughing at his expense you must be willing to part with something to compensate him. After all, that will be paying for the concert he is putting on for you."

"He is not asking to be compensated."

"He is not asking you to laugh. If he caught you laughing, he would drag you to the chief, and you know what that entails. It is not as if you can travel far in the car without a proper road, even if it is driving on grass. Look at Navi. You have to think more carefully, you know, like being deliberative.

What you have said can be considered an insult, and you know the consequences of that..."

"Giving up a sheep. I heard he gave a sheep to ask Kuku's grandmother to cover up her chest when the missionaries came here to visit them."

"He was very young. What was the point?"

"He paid after he began to grow his own crops. "

"He was insulting the integrity of mama. Someone has to mind relationships. They would have done the same if he had asked a child to cover up."

"What I am saying is that trees in the way of a vehicle have to be cut down, whether it is your grandfather's or some other tree."

"That is something to think about. The question then becomes, is it our duty to reconcile the idea of making way for a vehicle and preserving our vegetation?"

"I hope you are not asking that we sacrifice sheep in preparation."

"It is not a marriage that is necessary if not profitable. If anything, it is a building to replace people, it is not like replacing people with people. If a steel vehicle stands where vegetation should be, that is not replacing life with life."

"It is not as if all available vegetation is food, at this point we still have weeds in abundance and empty spaces with horse grass where we step repeatedly. It is time to study all of the vegetation around us and find out which properties are useful for our survival otherwise, they are nothing but weeds and they must be cut down to make room for vehicles among other things."

"Savor would have suggested that we offer a sheep for disposing of them unceremoniously, but my mother would probably have said we shouldn't get used to it."

Devie continued to echo his mother's words as they started packing their bags.

#

A silhouette of a man appeared in the path leading to Vidzietor's house, and he squinted to see who it was. The person spoke as he drew nearer to the house, asking permission to enter, "Agoo."

"Travelling this late, Savor?" Vidzietor asked.

"Yes, I am travelling because the matter is urgent. I understand that the children are leaving in the morning. They cannot leave until this matter has been dealt with."

"What, are you saying the children have been summoned to appear before the elders?"

"Yes," Savor emphasised the resolve and left.

Devie moved quickly to the door and listened to the parents speaking to each other in quiet tones.

"So this cannot wait?" Vidzienor asked with a sigh.

Devie called Vidzie.

"Hmmm?" Vidzie answered grudgingly.

When it was dawn, Vidzietor knocked at the children's door. He called out to the children saying, "You might as well unpack. You have a meeting with the elders."

Devie and Vidzie exchanged looks.

Vidzietor sounded doleful, "Hurry, perhaps, you can still travel early."

#

The elders gathered in Togbe's house looked grim.

"A matter has come to our attention. It is a matter of the destruction of a very important tree," Amator let them in on the trouble they are facing, "Vidzie, would you tell us what happened?"

Vidzie tried to recount the story of how he tried to park his car under a tree that was beside his father in law's house, "I was pulling the *whuu* vehicle into the compound. I pulled it under the tree, but as it turned out, there wasn't enough room..."

Adufie: "We want to know who you informed about bringing such a thing into the village?"

Vidzie: "It is a vehicle..."

Adufie: "It is not for understanding that people destroy shade trees."

Anayitor: "It is necessary to start over. Isn't that what we have to do?"

Amator: "We will need a sheep."

Vidzietor: "What did you say?"

*Adufi*e: "It must be a sheep."

"He was angry about the tree," Vidzienor observed as they walked away. That tree was planted by their grandfather. She wondered if he was pacified.

Vidzie: "When he was talking last evening, I thought..."

Devie: "My grandfather has said nothing."

Vidzie: "It is only a tree. It is not even a fruit tree. It has no purpose."

Vidzienor breaks into song, "*Atiade menye. Nye me tsea ku O. Gake me doa vorvorli.*" I am not a fruit bearing tree. I am a shadow giving tree.

Devie: "These big trees keep the *anyigba* earth from warming too much and the *ke* soil from washing away."

Vidzie: "Houses do that."

Devie: "They don't have leaves."

Vidzietor: "Putting together a road should be easy, but we have to take some things into consideration. First of all, the thing dug up our horse grass and left tire tracks, it will continue to dig into the ground unless we pad it. Also, it broke tree branches, the thing cannot move without running into trees.

We have to cut those down trees ourselves, but it is the beginning of the harmattan season, the ground is dry, tree branches are dry."

Vidzienor: "They shed their branches because the anyigba is colder. They will grow them again. Vidzie has given us firewood. A meeting has been called, but I still don't know why."

Vidzietor: "Perhaps. It is because the tree would have been killed before its time. The thing that has been laid on the grounds of the schoolhouse and the big road is grey salt."

#

It was *worle*, after the evening meal when everyone went out to clear the land for the new road to parallel the asphalt road which was still one hundred yards away separating the din of running engines from the first house at the front of the town. The new way was to run through the space behind the homes. Togbe suggested that they cut down as few trees as possible, and cut out space that was big enough to let the vehicle through.

Early in the morning with axes in hand, men cut down vegetation. They arranged the logs into a pile which kept the grass and shrubbery stunted.

Tomtom and rain fell as birds hovered near the ground. While the pile of wood prevented grass from growing, termites nibbled at the wood, and slowly, they rot away. Mama was the first to notice the gathered crawlers making the logs their home. Worms also continued to crawl whenever it rained, but other crawlers: beetles, ants and snakes hid under the logs. Then older people removed them and they became fuel for cooking.

Their elders in Agudze called another meeting after the second rainy season, just before the harmattan season. Togbe spoke up again and said there was too much shifting of the foot, and decisions were being made that took them in different directions. "People who dart their eyes from pavilion to yard fall a step behind," he said. He suggested that the lorry tyres be allowed to roll in the mud, but driving on the grass would kill it. Vidzietor suggested that they try the way the school does it. The school flattened the ground and covered the grass.

#

On a clear day in the evening, the people walked down the road towards the mountain behind the market. Prancing antelopes watched them with curiosity as they climbed the mountain. With their "jiggas" in hand, they went towards a big hole.

"This thing looks like salt," Vidzietor warned. He called it *kpalakpala*

"I am sure it was what they used," *Adufie* said.

The men dug up the rocks, and piled them in the baskets aluminium and brass basins. Some of the women took out the basins that were used in their marriage rites and lined them with some worn clothes. They dug up rocks and filled their baskets. Women and children carried them on their heads. Then carefully, they walked down the mountain. They piled them behind Vidzietor's house when they arrived home.

Before they could spread them on the ground construct the road, it was planting season and the rains began to fall.

Not long after, Mama had a dream. Mama told her dream to the women at the market. The community woke up to a shining and slippery road that made it impossible for them to walk anywhere, unable except behind their houses to go to market or to farm. It was Devienor who complained first. She complained that her *dzeveti* and other shrubbery and twigs were wilting despite the rainfall. Kukunor also complained. She added that rocks in the ground were exaggerated under the layer of crystals as the rains continued to fall. Horse grass was absent on the walkways, it was a fact that was not lost on anybody. As the rains continued to fall the crystals disappeared completely, but then a bigger problem ensued, the shrubbery and trees began to die everywhere. "There is a reason why rock is buried in the earth," Mama concluded.

"What is it exactly?" Sikanor asked.

"It is something in the salt family. Basalt was written on the pole beside the pit," Navi said.

"And you told this to whom?" Amanor asked.

Sikanor said something when she returned home. Devienor said that Navi knew something about it indeed, and she told her sister about it. They called a meeting.

"That does not happen to the ground or vegetation at the school," *Adufie* tried to reassure everyone.

"Perhaps we should use burnt clay and build the road just like we build homes, pots and stoves," Devietor suggested.

Sikator said that the ground would crack under the weight of the *whuu* vehicle, but they would give it a try, "We face the problem of finding other surfacing material. I think it is time we found out why the crystal at the school has not vanished."

Savor contributed some sheep to the people who lived behind the walls, so they took some sheep to the person at the gate.

"Thank you," the man said and closed the gate.

"Have you noticed that the ground is dirtier than the rocks we have?" *Adufie* asked as they walked away.

"Are you certain they used crystals? I have been thinking that our crystals look a little more like salt. We don't have any of the sticky black plastic that melts when it is hot either. Navi had told her sister that there was writing on a piece of flat wood that read "salt,"" Devietor revealed some information.

"Why didn't she say anything? Let's call her in," Kukutor clobbered with glee.

Navi arrived with her sister by her side.

"Tell the men what you told me," her sister nudged her and she gabbled.

"I greet you," Navi said on bended knees.

"Sit down, sit down," Devietor said excitedly, "Tell us about the salt."

"I just thought I saw writing on a stick beside the pit."

"So it didn't say salt," Devietor said grimly.

"Ahhh," *Adufie* grunted, "I would have known it."

Navi remembers seeing "Basalt" on a post a few feet from the entrance, but then there were other words on the board.

"I saw some pieces remain after the salt melted. They looked clouded and hard like the gray clay we eat," Mama continued.

"She speaks of clay that was found where her grandmother was born. Those are found where your grandmother was born," Togbe said in exasperation.

"She speaks of shale. There is a difference between basalt and shale," Kukutor said.

"Is that why we are losing our herbs? Let us not play with this," Mama scolded.

"Perhaps, we should talk to the people at....," Vidzietor began to say.

"The school. We will when they come to thank us for the sheep," *Adufie* completed the sentence.

"I am standing on it," Mama said. Togbe followed suit. One by one they left the meeting.

Chapter 8

"Shouldn't an ill person feel relief after vomiting? I have vomited and vomited, but nothing has changed."

"When was the last day you left the house....? Vidzienor asked, and Devie understood that Vidzienor hinted at pregnancy. Her mother-in-law explained that it took time for a mother to adjust to pregnancy. It was called finding hardship. Devie *fo fu*. She was found suffering when a seed implanted in her. She didn't understand the discomfort she felt.

"This way?" She asked.

"Quiet, she will hear you," her mother-in-law showed her seed of patience, self control, joy and tolerance.

For nine months, Devie carried herself and another. She never complained again. Devienor and Vidzie's mother kept her under close watch ever since her first encounter with excess.

#

Devie began to plan her activities at the market, three meals during the day, paying for the new iron strainer ladle that was pushed on her the previous week, a little extra money to be tied into her over cloth, little gifts for new babies and so on. Little did she know she was going to have the busiest dawn of her life. She was gripped by the work of pregnancy, so she began to feel unbearable pain in her abdomen. Vidzienor was sleeping when she heard her scream. Immediately she got ready for the arrival of the baby when the baby voluntarily separated from the womb. The baby slept. It appeared she woke, cried, ate and slept again. This happened every two hours. Devie slowly got used to waking up every two hours. She fed the infant, checked and changed the worn cloth that lay under her. Devie's mother and Vidzie's mother washed layettes every morning. People visited her and asked about the welfare of the baby. People called Devie Vidzienor. Her new name lasted seven days until the baby received a name. No one came empty handed. Devienor prepared akatsa for Devie to eat and she put spices into it.

Grandmothers gave baths to infants, stroking little bodies with *luffa* sponges, and tickled babies twisted themselves as if they were dancing. Vidzienor administered the first posture exercises to the infant with the first bath when she gently pushed on her joints and limbs with a soft towel. By the time she was able to think independently, the child was not only imbued with the habit of daily baths, but a sense of image one had to maintain. Grandmothers didn't have a set time for calisthenics, they encouraged exercises everywhere all the time. The exercise regime continued to be administered by aural means with calls to hold your head up, do not to support your chin on the palm of your hand, hold your mouth, pull up a chair and so on, so that an adult reflexively straightened up when one's name was called. Stretching came naturally especially with yawning.

#

They got up before daybreak for the outdoor ceremony, and worked in the darkness with a lamp. It was the day the infant was introduced to the world. There was also a naming ceremony and the entire village community was invited. Pouring libations to the ancestors was central to the ceremony. She was placed on the ground for a second to experience the hard earth, but she would not touch it again for another five months when she began to sit up. A child was not allowed to look into the eyes of adults, but it was not as if the newborn baby could see the adults looking down at her from the ground. After the ceremony she would be exposed to the outside world without her face being covered. She would be taken outside still protected from the sun. Devie's mother went outside early in the morning or early in the evening only. She was always in the company of one or more of the mothers.

Chapter 9

"I am going to Ademai," Sika told Sikanor.

"You also?"

"Yes."

"When are you going?"

"Next week."

"What are you going to eat? It is not as if you will get a piece of land and plant something before the food we give you to take along runs out, but you know we will follow you on the road. We will bring ground meals and ripe fruits and vegetables."

Sika knew that they would ask any driver going towards the city about her and stand by the road to get feedback everyday, "I will not have to grow crops. They are stored in "go" containers just like the ones Navi sells at the market. The people who live behind walls take those things along with them wherever they go."

"I have asked the question. Where is their farm?"

#

Sika visited the school when she returned. She wanted to see if changes had been made to the structure since she left. Like those she saw in the city, the school had resident hostels, classrooms and some other facilities. The day's session was closing, and teachers were walking towards the homes which were only hundreds of feet from the classrooms. Most of the teachers were men, there was one woman among them. She wore long knickers and a shirt just like the men. Her shirt also tucked into long knickers.

Sika went to the school offices to greet the secretary, "I am visiting you out of curiosity since I don't have to report to work until Monday."

"It is a good thing that you are here. Monday is when you resume duty. We have housing available for you, but you must sign the forms. You must bring your husband along to sign them," the lady insisted.

Sika thought about the papers the magistrate gave her and Kuku. She had not spoken to Kuku since that day. She went home.

The sun had set. Sikanor and Sika sat by the dying fire. They talked as they laid fish on the grid and turned it. Sika told her mother about the day she ran into Kuku.

Kuku was walking on the path between the school and the residences when he heard footsteps and turned to look behind and saw Sika. He stopped suddenly and began to whisk his feet backwards through the grass on the median.

"Can we walk together?" He asked when he fell in step with her. His voice was raspy.

Sika was taken aback, and she snapped, "You know what they say about evil coming into *gborme* the village, unwrapping its head when people are asking when you will select a woman."

"I want to tell you what I heard last night. Devie is pregnant," Kuku engaged her in conversation.

"Yes! I know."

"My father told my mother that the school still needs a cook."

"Yes!"

"My father says anyone can do it, but the person must fill out something called an application."

"Yes."

"I have a form for you to fill out."

Sika stopped in her tracks and stared at the form that had been filled out.

"We don't have birth certificates, but the woman at the office has agreed to issue a baptismal certificate instead. The woman who gave me the forms said you must promise to be married by the time you finished the course."

"To whom? No one has asked my father for my hand in marriage."

"You don't have to have anyone ask for your hand on this occasion. There was a magistrate at the place. We will go to his office and he will give you a piece of paper. You have to do it today.

"What do I tell my parents?"

"That you are going to the school."

Kuku and Sika entered a room where a scruffy old strange man was sitting on a wooden chair behind a small wooden table in the front left corner.

"We are ready," said a strange woman who entered the room after Sika and Kuku. It was the secretary who gave Kuku the application papers, he explained to Sika. He told her she was there to witness the ceremony. Sika nodded.

"When the man asks you any questions, answer yes," the woman told her.

Sika followed after Kuku. She answered a few questions, and the man gave them a piece of paper.

"We have all of the necessary information in our hands," the secretary said as she took the paper from Kuku.

Kuku and Sika went home.

Her mother listened, fidgeting all the while. Alas, she could not contain herself any longer. Her scream brought Sikator running to the fireplace. Sikanor told him that the people behind the walls thought that Sika and Kuku were married, so Sikator began to pace back and forth and mutter to himself after hearing the story, "Eii, you have laid down a proverb. Does Kukutor know? He wouldn't have told us even if he knew. Do we tell the elders first or confront him? I don't know what I might do."

"I think it is between the two of them. I will not say anything about it. This certainly calls for sheep, and Kukutor will have to see to it that it is given."

"Bring him here along with his father and question them both. He wouldn't come. Take it to the elders."

"You are forgetting that the school will find out that it is a lie."

"She is making us her accomplices now."

"Parents are always accomplices."

"Kuku has gone to the farm. You have our permission to catch him on the way back."

"To do what?"

"I will speak to his father at dawn."

"Is it a woman who asks for the hand of a man?"

"His son is already married."

"Ahhh. If you put it that way. I don't want him to speak to her until after drinks have been exchanged. He is going away tomorrow."

"Where will he go?"

"He will have to hide in his house."

"It has to be done before Monday. Her duties resume on Monday."

#

Kukutor was one of the first people from his community to learn how to read and write, and he became the head teacher. Every member of his household had clout in this community because of that, but there was an age at which a person must retire from teaching duties. Kukutor had passed that age. Kukutor no longer taught at the school. He worked on his farm. When Kuku was younger, Kukutor showed off shoes that were made in Germany and told the child that he had a given German name which was Fritz.

Their small village was not far from the equatorial shoreline, and it was located one hour west of the Greenwich meridian. Missionaries from Germany arrived decades earlier in the mid-nineteenth century to set up communities that had markets, churches and schools. They encouraged the people they met to convert to their way of living. While they preached the proper way to prepare for a life in the kingdom of God, their lives on earth were lived within the framework of the German lifestyle. Converts learned how to read and write, and to manage their community through the distribution of goods and services.

When war broke out between Germany and other nations, the British crown totally destroyed everything that was German, then took over the administration of the land where Agudze was as it slowly expanded its authority. Everything that was German was replaced by everything that was British. Men were encouraged to go to war on behalf of Britain as British citizens when war broke out again between Germans and Britons. Local languages survived because Germans had encouraged people to worship God in the vernacular.

After the second war, the indigenous peoples began to agitate for self rule. However, the new ways of life they had adopted remained and competed with the old ways of living.

#

Kukutor thrust his shoulders through the window frame and rested his elbows on the sill to take in the *fornli* (dawn) fresh air until he was ready to eat his morning meal. He walked to the side of the house, and standing astride the horse grass median in the walkway, he took water into his mouth from a calabash he held in one hand, standing in the walkway.

Someone walked towards the house. He moved behind a cashew tree with water still in his mouth and watched the silhouette of the man walk where he had stood. Kukunor called out Sikator's name before he could ask, "Who is it?" Kukutor drew nearer and stood behind the wall to hear the conversation between them. He struggled to keep his lips closed as water came out of his mouth in spurts. Sikator said he had something to say to Kukutor. Kukunor said she would tell him when he returned. Kukutor came out after Sikator had left. He went to visit him after his return from the farm. Sikator and Kukutor talked between themselves in Sikator's home.

Sikanor tried to assure her husband, "It is not as if she will not live in a beautiful house. Besides, Devie does not live in a house that is beautiful. If only Devie's parents had not allowed anyone else to marry her."

"I am beginning to think you planned this thing so that you can live in one of those houses."

"That is not what I am saying."

"Everyone loves a good thing. Have you seen the way Vidzietor has walked since his son brought a car? Our daughter is going to live behind those walls and he will get us a car?"

"What I hear is they have agreed to marry her. Even the people who live behind walls think she must not live there alone."

#

Savor opened the gate of the fence in the morning and the quadrupeds wandered off to the *adame* where grass grew in abundance before Kukutor stopped by to give him the news.

Living was performing traditional duties mindlessly from day to day. Time moved with every breath. If a person continued breathing, it would come to pass. The only preparation was found in tradition. Along with people died ideas that carried them on unless their children carried on these ideas, they were as good as dead. They were embracing a world that was not theirs, so they asked permission and gave thanks. If an idea was not tested, if the idea was not meant for their survival, they were as good as dead. If those two did not continue to follow tradition, their children would be lost.

Adufie was walking on his verandah when he saw them. He stopped and watched his neighbours speak to each other. After a while, he interrupted the conversation to offer his greetings, then he paused as if to gather his thoughts. *Adufie* watched his neighbours speak to each other for some time. He heard rumours without eavesdropping necessarily, because people spoke loudly here. *Adufie* understood that Kukutor was preparing for the marriage celebration between his son and his neighbour, Sikator's daughter.

He interrupted the conversation again saying, "Isn't this some trouble? You could have used fowl instead of spending hard earned money on sheep. Why buy two of them when we are all but a few people? Look, having too much food breeds nothing but illness."

Kukutor cast a disapproving look at his neighbour and bellowed, "You know you are just speaking for the sake of making conversation. You know why we have to get two sheep."

Adufie was astounded and blurted out, "Ah! I was at a meeting of elders. I thought it was a suggestion, it was not to be done on suspicion!"

Amator convened the meeting, "Good morning to you all, I am sure you have heard why we are here?"

"Good morning," everyone responded.

Amator continued, "We are asking for two sheep before the ceremony. For now, we contend with appealing to an abortee, a fornicatee or their creator if either or both of the children have conducted themselves in such a manner as to commit such an aberration. Moreover, others will become aware that all it takes to undo a problem is to sacrifice sheep if we publicise our intent. Some people will wonder and gossip. And disposing of a person in an improper manner after pre-marriage consummation of passion be it with or without consequences that is *nugbegble,* that is waste. They will be mounting the problem with a lie if we ask."

Sikator cringed at the thought of anyone calling his daughter a liar. He said nothing. However, there was an extended discussion among the elders. Amator reminded everyone, "A few oil palm trees must be felled to produce wine for this occasion. Palm fronds also must be shaved from these oil palm trees to make roof covers for logs and stakes, so that people will jubilate in the shade. Non-fruit-bearing trees grow in abundance in *aveme*. Some larger *mle* hearths will be needed. Red clay is found near Agudze, but people prefer to mould red clay into drinking pots. There are young people in the village. Collections of dry twigs and other dead wood that have fallen on the ground are very light, and carrying them as they return home after a walk to the *bome* (farm) is part of their daily activities. Sometimes, twigs are bound together with willow and sold at the market."

Anayitor spoke up, "I don't want to cut you short, but it should be done tomorrow. They will have the sheep slaughtered at their feet quietly, and the prayers said quietly. The idea to replace a plant whenever one is uprooted, what has become of it? People beat around the bush. We have to know what to do to not overreach. I don't quite understand what you mean by with or without consequences. Once a person gives in to passion, a line has been crossed, whether it results in conception or not. Wouldn't you say that fornication is better than abortion by far? The big issue is preparation prior to consummation. Marrying is without consequences. Not marrying has consequences. Some who believe in reincarnation say it is possible for an abortee, who is ejected from the womb prematurely, to be reincarnated where he finds a home, and a fornicatee, that one whose vulva is open prematurely will be married. One must not judge differences by degrees or the extent of attempt at disposal."

Sikator cried in pain, "Ultimately, it is about the people who are involved. It is never easy to hide these things, because culprits have to deal with loss associated with abortion and fornication. It's such a grievous crime. Vodada acted against the interest of a parent. Wo-e! Where does this come from?"

Woe is a reference to pain. Literally speaking, a person has an encounter with pain. Pain is personified in these parts, and a struggle with pain brings little enjoyment. People had these experiences. That was what people talked about. Some were dissenting while others were agreeing, but they were all excited and energized.

Adufie brought the conversation back to the present saying, "By the way, my point is no one has seen either of them engage in any such behaviour. Have you asked?" *Adufie* spoke up trying to convince Kukutor.

Sikator pressed his palms against his temples as if to steady his mind. He responded, "Even if I suspect such a thing of my daughter, my suspicion will not be confirmed until after the ceremony."

"People must not do things just because they can," *Adufie* scoffed at the idea, looking indignant.

The livestock farmer waved his arms and said, "In order to remove lice, you are removing your heads. It was suggested, either he would follow or he wouldn't."

The story was told of a lady who got so irritated by the idea of lice breeding in her hair and crawling on her scalp that she took off her head in order to remove them. Stories were woven into conversations.

Adufie repeated himself, saying, "We must not do things because we can."

Kukutor scratched his head and walked towards the trees outside his compound in search of a steady post on which to fasten securely the fidgeting rams, and *Adufie* walked on.

#

Kuku and his mother walked together on their way home after the ceremony. He hunched his shoulders, trudged and quipped, "I have heard that they slaughtered goats at their feet. Devie must not be good after all."

His mother looked surprised. She said absent-mindedly, "I didn't think that they would go through with it."

"What do you mean?"

"It was discussed at the meeting of elders when news broke that you asked for her hand in marriage."

"What was discussed?"

"The possibility of the two of you being fornicators and abortionists. Someone suggested that you offered two sheep to cover such misdeeds."

"Perhaps we were, but the sheep had nothing to do with it."

"Perhaps it is to show that bad actions affect others negatively."

"The poor sheep."

"Those who do such things bear a loss," she protested, appearing distressed. Kuku looked at his mother questioning. "Those who give others away unceremoniously, an abortee and fornicatee are human too," she whined.

Adufie listened as he walked behind them. He fell in step with them after a while and began a conversation with Kukutor. They stepped a few feet ahead of Kuku and his mother, and *Adufie* asserted himself, "I want to talk to you about the people who live their lives behind walls."

"You must be referring to the visitors who make their living in buildings, priests and clerks?"

"Yes. They have gates or have only one door even to their homes. They must be afraid of the world."

"They go outside to bring it inside."

"No one has ever seen them in the market."

"They use the *torwhuu*. They came on those and settled on the coast. They built houses on the coast first. They continue to bring food on the *torwhuu* even now. They have distribution centers behind the walls. They have markets, post offices and so on, that is where clerks work."

"This must have been before the *yamewhuu*," *Adufie* said, reflecting on what Vidzie said months before.

Kuku walked away when *Adufie* began to speak. He walked towards home appearing to be preoccupied. It was as if he was aware that his father's house was at the end of the winding path yet getting there in a daze, only vaguely was he aware of everything along the path, perhaps he was drawn by *Adufie*'s probing speeches. He was not out of earshot.

#

Sikator woke up at the first cockcrow. He lay in bed staring at the ceiling. The second cockcrow came to pass. After a long silence, he heard footsteps. "He's here," he said. He jumped and dashed for Sika's door. Just then a man entered the compound. He was wearing a dark red hunter's smock and his face was smeared with some greenish concoction. Sika came out of the room, and immediately the man reached for her arm and dragged her outside the compound. Kukutor rushed and untied the ram from a tree, doubled up his steps and caught up with them while dragging sheep behind him. Together they walked to the chief's compound. Kuku was already there. He was standing between his father and another executioner. The executioners dug up some soil with points on their long knives, then they motioned to the fathers to place the necks of the sheep over the pits. The executioners held on to the rams' heads while the fathers bound their limbs together. Everything was still. As the cock crew for the third time in the morning, the men slaughtered and drained the sheep. After that, they left. The children walked away with their fathers in silence.

Chapter 10

A large fence separated those buildings from the village. As Sikanor walked around it, a man came out of an opening in the fence. She greeted him, she remembered it was the man who had been to the market to give Devie the letter a long time before. The man went behind the fence and she followed him, walking through the gate.

"What are you going to do here with us?" the man asked.

"My daughter lives here, that is why I have come."

The man rubbed his cheeks with his index finger and asked, "Which one is she? Now let me see, I have seen her walking with you, she is a young woman, she has just started working here." With his finger pointing towards the buildings beyond the asphalt covered drive, he directed her, "Walk up this road to the first building at the end, she lives near it, not beside it, but facing it. I think she is at work, but she will be out at noon."

Sikanor knew embracing another style of living required preparation, she knew wearing a different type of clothing required instruction. Even if she was willing to take instruction, she was yet to take instructions from children especially when it was given by example. Doing so would be abandoning the code of conduct set forth in Agudze. She knew she had to prepare her daughter to make the transition into adulthood according to the rules of Agudze, so she sat down with her daughter and gave her a talk about what to wear to the ceremony bearing in mind that choosing proper clothes was part of preparation. If it were up to Sika she would have worn a school dress to the ceremony just like her friends would have done.

Kuku answered when Sikanor knocked on the door at noon. He offered her a seat and some water to drink.

"I hear Sika is here at noon."

"Not always, I will get her if you wait."

Sikanor sat on a stone slab on a veranda overlooking flower beds in the yard of the detached house while Kuku walked to the side of the clubhouse where Sika was cooking and motioned for her to come out. Sika waved through the glass windows when she saw him. He sat on one of the chairs outside and waited, fidgeting, digging the earth with his toes. A man who had the telltale signs of a priest was also sitting on the veranda. Furthermore, he waved to Kuku to come over and sit beside him after asking his permission to do so.

"Do you have a minute," he asked Kuku and engaged him in conversation.

Sika could come out soon. "Women are unpredictable," Kuku said.

"There are lessons one must learn in order to move from one stage in life to another. If you narrow your focus you will find that she is a progeny and a progenitor. Narrow your focus further and you will find in her a companion who shares by accident your weaknesses and vituperation or your strengths and wealth like a sister being contaminated by a rotten seed.

That is why marriage is a community affair. If you see it through your eyes alone, you might as well call it something else."

"Something that is unpredictable."

"A seed will not grow under certain conditions. A bad seed has limitations. It may grow if its limitations are overcome by essence, however. We all have limitations. A shriveled seed will grow if it has life in it. You have watched parents complain about doing everything for a seedling, propping it up, watering it and so on."

"What do you mean?"

"Focusing on the task rather than the performer is prejudicial, just as focusing on the person rather than the performer is prejudicial. The missing link in this argument is the performer. If you focus on the performer you either ignore both task and person or appreciate both task and person, it is not tipping the scales in favour of one or the other."

"What has that to do with a woman? She is not a seedling. She is an adult."

"Your task is to help bring out the essence of womanhood. What she is as a person is determined by you. You cannot draw out her potential, she must yield. Salt melts under certain conditions."

"I wonder what makes the sun give off rays?"

"A man is like soil and he provides conditions for a woman to either thrive or die. You provide the environment for her to thrive, comfort and security, although you yourself and she must get something that comes from beyond. I am sure you understand that. It is your mother or sister's responsibility to discuss such things with you. That is why a wife is called a man's mother and a husband is called a woman's father."

Marriage is about taking proper possession, getting everyone involved in the process.

"It still does not explain why women change."

"It does. Women respond to the message they are given in their environment, they are constantly comparing the new with the old within themselves. They change, but their essence will not. You must learn about their needs and potential. If you asked me, since there are subtle variations in women, you must stick with one."

"What do people do when they do not agree?"

"We celebrate disagreement because we look for new facts, but there are no new facts. We ought to celebrate the facts by saying and saying again what fact there is in our own way."

"We do. Teacher Yawo says it is stating the obvious over and over again."

The priest gave Vidzie a copy of a book. He glanced through it as the priest returned to his seat. It had several aphorisms but one reminded him of what *Adufie* said, that a woman was what a man made of her. The ideas of the priest simply reinforced what his elders had taught, or at least were trying to teach him.

#

Sikanor had been on a mission to make Sika understand a few things since she came across Kukunor and heard that Kuku told his mother that he and Sika didn't share the same bed.

"He has to wait," Sikanor said, "Most men wait." She thought they had their lives together until Kukunor said that Kukutor said the magistrate could give them a piece of paper and make them have separate lives.

"Who will take them back? Kukutor will not allow him to go back home," Kukunor assured Sikanor.

"She will not be allowed to be sent back either," Sikanor affirmed her resolve.

#

"I don't know what they are thinking?" Kuku pouted after Sikanor left, "They are planning another function. That is all you do, plan functions when you should be cooking. What did your mother tell you to do?"

"My mother does not have to deal with these duties. Did you say you were going to spend time on the farm? Perhaps you will not be tired of doing nothing," she added as an afterthought, "Perhaps you can be a clown at the function." She walked into the inner room and came out with an outfit that was made from two different types of cloth. One side was bright and plain but on the other was dark cloth with patterns, "You have to cover your head with a headdress which is made from dyed cotton wool." The wig she showed had the appearance of dyed hair colour fading back to gray, "You know that hair becomes multiple coloured in between. You have to put *akalo* on your face also."

"Am I going to kill anything?" He asked, "I want to live not work."

"You are going to sing and wave your arms in the air like a bird."

"Men don't wear sasa. When our neighbour who lives to the right of us visited, he said we were only allowed to plant flowers in the backyard of the house. I say there are no dependent fools like us. Then he struck up a conversation and was rather talkative when he asked about my parents."

"He knows your father."

"Yes. I asked him if he thought God heard prayers here since we left all of the food he created for us behind in the village. He tried to say that it was not very different from living in the village. How is that? I ask. He wanted to help me become more active in the community and thought I should go to the city and take a course also. He said I could become a clerk which would take up to seven years of study."

Sika was silent for a second, but she relented, "It is up to you."

"He said it cost money," Kuku continued.

"We cannot buy a car if we use what we have," Sika didn't see the prospect of Kuku obtaining a scholarship to study in the city.

"The trouble I have with the whole thing is that no one even grows food here. Where does the food come from, and who is growing it? I have been thinking that I should walk back to the village in the morning and work on my father's farm, or mine if they haven't given away the land."

There was a knock on the door. Kuku walked to the door and was surprised, "We just called your name?" Kuku's parents came to visit them, and he offered them seats. Sika brought water for them to drink.

"It was difficult to find the place. No one sat outside, as we went knocking on several doors...in daylight, mind you, looking for your place, and a man peered through a wall to see us just like you did before he opened the door."

Before the children could acknowledge her observation, she asked why the elementary school looked different from the one they had attended. Kuku explained that children in elementary school were young so they had to be taken care of by adults.

"You are the adults here, and you have become parents as the children have become brothers and sisters."

"What do you mean?" Kuku asked.

"It's as if he doesn't know," Kukunor sneered, "They give you food. You help them. You get married without telling us. We have now become visitors in the home of our children."

"This does not absolve us of our duties as parents," Kukutor said, "I think we are just as confused as the children."

"The children sit around doing nothing. What is that resort? What happens when they grow, do these adults follow them into the future?"

Kuku tried to soften her demeanor with an invitation, "Nana, you can come and stay with us and take care of your grandchildren."

"That is grandchildren, you must remember that!" Kukunor retorted. She eyed Sika from the corner of her eyes.

Sika winced in the kitchen. Sometimes women treat a person well until she becomes a daughter. "Have you informed your parents about the good news? Kuku, about the possibility of you going to the city?" She asked.

"She is going with him. We should assume that they will go together. It has been a long time, Kuku," Kukunor demanded a grandchild, glaring at Kuku, "You have to send us news when she is pregnant, perhaps we will visit then."

"I think he wants to go alone," Kukutor teased, for it was obvious that they would leave together.

"Absolutely not!" Kukunor cried.

"You say that because you want to have your grandchild. We do not change things."

"He has allowed his child to walk into the fire," Kukunor muttered under her breath.

Kuku told them about his decision to go to the village to farm a piece of land, but his father immediately discouraged him saying Vidzie built a petrol filling station on the land. He broached the idea of taking cans of food from Sika since she told Devie that she had some cans in stock.

"So this is not about children," Sika breathed a sigh of relief. She returned from the kitchen with a box full of provisions.

Kuku offered to carry it home for his parents. On the way, they talked about the changes in the village. Kuku learned they had a clinic. Vidzie also opened a store to sell the wares that he brought from Ademai. Several other trees were removed to pave the way for the streets. Kukutor added that they were turning the community into Ademai. He argued that Agudze was not a coastal area, "What difference does that make? God is everywhere. The journey into independence begins with a blessing. He blesses men with children, food, a place to live, clothing and protection, and he gives instructions. Do we have to bury the living earth as well?"

#

It was *fornli* just before the sun rose and birds sang their worship. They flew high, perched on branches and pecked at insects on tree barks. Birds singing is an invitation to rise, and no one asks people to get out of bed at dawn. People are prompted by bird calls to eat at specific intervals, mid-morning, noon and evening responding to the innate call to feed. Food is available to them all year round, they find food on almost any tree. Although there are some fruits that are poisonous, they eat all year round.

Kuku and Sika had another disagreement, but Kuku assured Sika, "I have been reading *The Joy of Communication*," as he walked towards the door.

"You are doing this thing again," Sika squirmed and drew him back to the room.

"What?"

"Showing me that I am thinking something that has been thought of by someone else."

"I am affirming your thoughts."

"Perhaps they need not be affirmed. You know as well as I that only one person's thought carries us all." Sika could not help but restart the discussion and cite the behaviour of birds to get Kuku to eat.

Kuku explained, "Food is what people here say it is. Children learn that palm kernels have great taste and stuff them into their mouths while cracking them for oil. They taste sweet whether raw or roasted. Before long however, children begin to realise that it is a childish thing to do."

Dawn does not yield enough light for human activity, it is time to listen to the world outside and to plan. The tendency to perform acts that promote continuity is very much part of the makeup of our being, although some of these acts are redundant.

#

They arrived to visit their parents in the village. It was just before the sun set when the sound of a car engine interrupted the sound of people pounding *fufu* with a pestle in mortar, also pepper, salt, onions and tomato being smashed with smooth cobbles. Kuku took the pestle from his mother and pounded the fufu until it was soft and smooth.

Sika began to wretch, and Kukunor said, "You have to stop working and start living."

After the evening meal, Kuku and Sika sat in the hall and had a conversation with Kukunor and Kukutor.

"What is your favourite book?" Kukutor asked.

"Ademai Tea Party," Kuku answered.

"Tell me why it is your favourite book?"

"It is alright to get rid of structures that are harmful."

"You agree that it is alright to keep a structure that is beneficial."

"I think so," he replied after giving it some thought.

"Tell us before you have a child, I must send your mother to teach you how to raise a child."

"Daycare is beneficial as you say. Children get a good start with the common language and education, the way things are today," Kuku explained.

"Grandparents only help out, so you have to spend time with your child. That is the benefit of it. It is only for a brief period of two to three years until a child weaned," Kukutor continued.

"I think we have to move all of you to live with us in the city," Kuku suggested.

"What is your father going to do in the city?" Kukunor wondered.

"We will think about that when the time comes, my son," Kukutor suggested.

"Do you have any stories?" Sika asked, "My father has said you have stories which must be told."

"Follow your mother-in-law around when the sun rises. It is time to go to bed now," Kukutor appeared to brush aside her request, but then he gave them a sermon, "God is everywhere. I don't think he expects us to be where he does not expect us to be. He is with us when we find ourselves alone, and even appoint others to help, but that may be an unnecessary charge. You must sweep the compound with your mother when you hear the cock crows the third time."

"What about an alarm clock that is set at 5:30, my father?" Sika asked.

"It is not as reliable as the dawn chorus," Kukutor answered.

"Oh, isn't this film like the one that we watched while we were staying with you?" Kukunor asked, looking away, "Do you remember that I said your television worked better than the one Vidzie had?"

"Vidzie's television received messages. The receptor was modified to receive messages from the transmitter to show more pictures and block other transmitters," Kuku explained.

"So now we can not watch anything, huh?"

www.ingramcontent.com/pod-product-compliance
Lightning Source LLC
Chambersburg PA
CBHW060617130626
46555CB00002B/537